folk STYLE

Innovative designs to knit
including sweaters, hats,
scarves, gloves, and more

folkSTYLE

Innovative designs to knit
including sweaters, hats,
scarves, gloves, and more

MAGS KANDIS

INTERWEAVE PRESS
www.interweave.com

PHOTOGRAPHY: Carol Kaplan
COVER AND INTERIOR DESIGN: Jillfrances Gray
TECHNICAL EDITING: Lori Gayle

Text © 2007 Mags Kandis
Photography and illustrations © 2007 Interweave Press LLC
All rights reserved.
Interweave Press LLC
201 East Fourth Street
Loveland, CO 80537-5655 USA
interweave.com

Printed and bound in China through Asia Pacific Offset

Library of Congress Cataloging-in-Publications Data

Kandis, Mags.

Folk style : innovative designs to knit including
sweaters, hats, scarves, gloves,
and more / Mags Kandis, author.
p. cm.
Includes index.
ISBN-13: 978-1-59668-020-3 (pbk.)
1. Knitting–Patterns. I. Title.
TT820.K257 2007
746.43'2041–dc22

2007015109

10 9 8 7 6 5 4 3 2 1

ACKNOWLEDGMENTS

I have always believed that you are only as good as the people who surround you. During this marvelous *Folk Style* journey—from conception to bookshelf—I have been surrounded by the best. . . .

Ann Budd for keeping me on track, taking on more than expected, and doing far more than she should have. I can never thank her enough for her ability to turn my sophomoric attempts of written English into words I can feel proud of.

Pam Allen, whose tremendous knowledge and kindness made me feel comfortable and competent in an unfamiliar place.

Linda Stark for the phone call that started it all.

Betsy Armstrong for welcoming me to Interweave Press with a big smile, fabulous energy, and Thai food.

Marilyn Murphy and Linda Ligon for their incredible curiosity, vision, and ingenuity.

Carol Kaplan and her assistant Denise for magically transforming what was in my head to a photograph.

The grace, patience, and brio of the models—Caitlin FitzGerald, Maureen Emerson, Angela Willey, Leslie Beattie, Elvia Beattie, Jo Lene McKenna, and Kaylee, Sydney, and Gracie Donovan.

The proprietors of KnitWit Yarn Shop and Coffee Bar in Portland, Maine. Anna and Joshua opened their doors to a whirl of kids and camera equipment on a blustery day offering welcomed warmth and cappuccinos.

Lisa Evans—and her fabulous brood, including Sam—for letting "strangers" break into her beautiful home for an impromptu photo shoot. Add to that an evening of "chowda" and fabulous conversation . . . I still tell the story!

All the talented designers whose innovative and unique translations of the word "folk" made my heart sing and my work easy.

The yarn companies for generously allowing us the opportunity to work with their gorgeous and inspiring yarns.

All of the talented and generous staff at Interweave Press for always making me feel I had a soft place to land if I were to fall.

CONTENTS

Folk Style is a melding
of cultures and eras . . .

WHAT IS FOLK STYLE?

Consider a classic Nordic Fair Isle with a fabulously shocking change of scale and hue, a graphic motif from the South Pacific craftily applied to modern hand warmers, a whisper of a wrap that collides with a patchwork quilt, or antique Indian crewelwork that "skirts the issue." These are just a few of the inspired designs in *Folk Style*—a melding of cultures and eras and a global interaction of color, texture, motif, and shape, all fashioned into knits with unmistakable folk components, yet undeniably contemporary style.

From the start, the vision for *Folk Style* was a gathering of global cultures and folk influences using knitting as the common thread. This collection of patterns celebrates our ever-shrinking world by creatively grabbing a soupçon of this and a smattering of that to reflect how fantastically diverse—yet strikingly similar—we are. Using folk references and ethnic motifs, shapes, and colors, we can produce a beautiful map of our world, a creative timeline of history, and, ultimately, a sensational knit that creates joy in the making and reflects personal style through its detailing.

In *Folk Style*, you will find an array of twenty-two handknitted projects, from small to large, easy to challenging, subdued to colorful, textural, and/or lacy. The projects reflect ideas and talents from sixteen designers who come from varying countries, backgrounds, and perspectives—from immigrant to tenth generation, young to . . . uh . . . mature, world explorer to armchair traveler. Some designs reflect folk traditions, ethnicity, and culture; others blur the boundaries and reflect

cultures that clash or bridge traditional and modern. Some designers drew upon their own history and pieced together the stories of their lives in their projects. Others took the opportunity to plunge into a heretofore unknown culture or era. The result? Each designer approached the concept of what is "folk" with individuality and, as has always been true with folk art and handcrafted textiles, each design reflects the unique personality of the maker.

The most important aspect of the "Style" series books (*Scarf Style*, *Wrap Style*, and *Lace Style*) is the Design Notebook, which begins on page 134 in *Folk Style*. Take some time to flip through the pages and get inspiration from the varied projects, then turn to the Design Notebook and learn how to develop your own ideas, including ways to gather inspirations, how to choose colors and work them into your knitting, and how to add surface embellishments in the folk tradition. The Design Notebook offers both novice and experienced knitters tips, hints, and suggestions on how to create a garment with a sense of folk style.

What is most engaging about knitting is its simplicity. For over a thousand years, across mountains and oceans, we have knitted the same way—save for a technique here and there. Still, all knitting is based on the same knit and purl stitches and how they are used in combination. The basic tools have always been the same—some pointed sticks, a bit of string, and an idea. You most likely have the first two—*Folk Style* gives you the third. So grab your needles and let's start traveling!

. . . each design reflects
the unique personality
of the maker.

folkPROJECTS

Browsing through a linens catalog, **Pam Allen** was taken by a red bedspread with blocks of rustic embroidery. "After I began the sweater, I received a postcard that showed an Andean woman knitting—she wore a jacket covered with embroidery and small white buttons. So the idea for the sweater took a turn in another direction," Pam confides. Adding embroidery to knitwear allows you to be spontaneous—no need to stay on a grid. And you can add lots of color without having to think about tangled balls of yarn or keeping an even tension.

BACK

With smaller needles, CO 72 (83, 94) sts. Knit 8 rows. Change to larger needles and work even in St st until piece measures 6½ (8, 9)" (16.5 [20.5, 23] cm) from CO, ending with a WS row. Mark each end of last row completed for base of armholes. Cont even in St st until piece measures 12 (14½, 16)" (30.5 [37, 40.5] cm) from CO, ending with a WS row. *Next row:* (RS) K23 (27, 30), BO center 26 (29, 34) sts for neck, knit to end—23 (27, 30) sts rem each side for shoulders. Place sts on holders.

LEFT FRONT

With smaller needles, CO 42 (47, 53) sts. Knit 8 rows. Change to larger needles. *Next row:* (RS) Knit to last 6 sts, pm, k6. *Next row:* (WS) Knit to marker, slip marker (sl m), purl to end of row. Cont working 6 sts at center front edge in garter st (knit every row) and rem sts in St st until piece measures 6½ (8, 9)" (16.5 [20.5, 23] cm) from CO, ending with a WS row. Mark side seam edge (beg of RS row) for base of armhole. Cont as established until piece measures 7½ (9, 10)" (19 [23, 25.5 cm) from CO and 1" (2.5 cm) above armhole marker, ending with a WS row.

Shape Collar

With RS facing, knit to m, M1 (see Glossary, page 155), sl m, k6—1 st inc'd. Work 7 rows even as established. Rep the shaping of the last 8 rows 3 (4, 4) more times, working new sts in St st—46 (52, 58) sts. Cont as established until piece measures 12 (14½, 16)" (30.5 [37, 40.5] cm) from CO, ending with a WS row. Place 23 (25, 28) sts at neck edge for collar on one holder, then place rem 23 (27, 30) sts at armhole edge on a separate holder for shoulder.

FINISHED SIZE

26 (30, 34)" (66 [76, 86.5] cm) chest circumference, buttoned. Cardigan shown measures 26" (66 cm).

YARN

DK weight (#3 Light).

Shown here: GGH Scarlett (100% cotton; 122 yd [112 m]/50 g): #14 red, 5 (7, 9) balls; #28 light green, #36 orange, and #35 aqua, 1 ball each.

NEEDLES

Body and sleeves—size 6 (4 mm). Edging—size 5 (3.75 mm). Adjust needle size if necessary to obtain the correct gauge.

NOTIONS

Markers (m); stitch holders; spare needle of any type in size 6 (4 mm) for three-needle bind-off; tapestry needle; three ⅝" (1.5 cm) buttons for front closure; about fifty assorted small white buttons ranging from ⅜" to ⅝" (1 to 1.5 cm; available at fabric stores); sharp-point sewing needle and matching thread for attaching buttons.

GAUGE

22 stitches and 31 rows = 4" (10 cm) in stockinette stitch on larger needles.

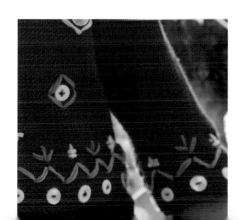

RIGHT FRONT

With smaller needles, CO 42 (47, 53) sts. Knit 6 rows.

Buttonhole Row 1: (RS) K3, yo twice, k2tog, k1, sl m, knit to end of row.

Buttonhole Row 2: (WS) Purl to m, k2, knit into first yo and drop loop of second yo from needle, k3. For the first buttonhole only, change to larger needles.

Buttonhole Row 3: K3, insert tip of right needle into buttonhole again and k1, k2, sl m, knit to end.

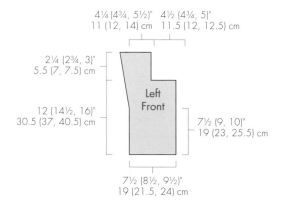

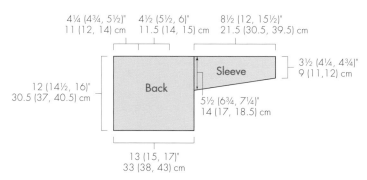

Next row: Purl to m, sl m, k6. *Cont working 6 sts at center front edge in garter st (knit every row) and rem sts in St st until piece measures 1½ (2¼, 2¾)" (3.8 [5.5, 7] cm) above previous buttonhole, ending with a WS row, then rep Buttonhole Rows 1–3; rep from * one more time to complete third buttonhole. *Tip:* Count the number of garter ridges between the first and second buttonholes so you can make the third buttonhole spaced the same distance above the second buttonhole. Cont as established until piece measures 6½ (8, 9)" (16.5 [20.5, 23] cm) from CO, ending with a WS row. Mark side seam edge (end of RS row) for base of armhole. Cont as established until piece measures 7½ (9, 10)" (19 [23, 25.5 cm) from CO and 1" (2.5 cm) above armhole marker, ending with a WS row.

Shape Collar

With RS facing, k6, sl m, M1 knit to end—1 st inc'd. Work 7 rows even as established. Rep the shaping of the last 8 rows 3 (4, 4) more times, working new sts in St st—46 (52, 58) sts. Cont as established until piece measures 12 (14½, 16)" (30.5 [37, 40.5] cm) from CO, ending with a RS row. Place 23 (25, 28) sts at neck edge for collar on one holder, then place rem 23 (27, 30) sts at armhole edge on a separate holder for shoulder.

Add detail and originality to stockinette stitch with embroidery and embellishments.

JOIN SHOULDERS

Place 23 (27, 30) held sts for left front and back shoulders on separate needles. Hold pieces tog with RS touching, WS of garment facing out. Use the spare needle and the three-needle bind-off method (see Glossary, page 152) to join left shoulder sts tog. Join right shoulder sts in the same manner.

SLEEVES

With larger needles and RS facing, pick up and knit 62 (74, 80) sts evenly spaced along front and back between armhole markers. Beg with a WS row, work 3 rows in St st. *Dec row:* (RS) K2, k2tog, work to last 4 sts, ssk, k2—2 sts dec'd. Rep Dec row every 4 rows 4 (0, 0) more times, then every 6 rows 6 (8, 2) times, then every 8 rows 0 (4, 11) times—40 (48, 52) sts rem. Work even until sleeve measures 7½ (11, 14½)" (19 [28, 37] cm) from pick-up row, ending with a RS row. Change to smaller needles. Knit 8 rows—sleeve measures about 8½ (12, 15½)" (21.5 [30.5, 39.5] cm) from pick-up row. With WS facing, BO all sts.

FINISHING

Collar

Return 23 (25, 28) held sts of left front collar to larger needles with RS facing and rejoin yarn to beg of sts, ready to work a RS row. *Next row:* (RS) M1, work in established patt to end—24 (26, 29) sts. Cont even as established until collar reaches to center back neck without stretching. BO all sts. Return 23 (25, 28) held sts of right front collar to larger needles with WS facing and rejoin yarn to beg of sts, ready to work a WS row. *Next row:* (WS) M1, work in established patt to end—24 (26, 29) sts. Cont even as established until collar reaches to center back neck without stretching. BO all sts. With yarn threaded on a tapestry needle, sew BO edges of collar tog at center back. Sew collar selvedge to neck edge.

Sew side and sleeve seams. With sewing needle and thread, sew front closure buttons to left front garter st band, opposite buttonholes on right front.

Embroidery

With double strand of green threaded on a tapestry needle and beg at first row of collar shaping on right front, work whipstitches (see Glossary, page 156) along garter st selvedge of collar, up around the back neck, and down to the first row of collar shaping on left front. Work a second line of whipstitches using a double strand of orange in a similar manner, but this time beg on the left front and end on the right front so the orange overcast sts slant in the opposite direction from the green sts and create a cross-stitch effect as shown in photograph. With double strand of aqua and beg about ½" (1.3 cm) above top buttonhole on right front, work a zigzag line of 1" (2.5 cm) straight sts just inside the garter st edging down the right front, around the lower body, and up the right front to end about ½" (1.3 cm) above the top button as shown. With double strand of aqua, work a zigzag line of straight sts around each cuff just above the garter st edging as shown. With double strand of green, work ½" (1.3 cm) cross-stitches (see page 148) oriented like plus signs at the peak of every other zigzag on body and sleeves. With double strand of orange, work a cluster of three ½" (1.3 cm) straight sts at each zigzag peak between the green cross stitches on body and sleeves. Fold collar back as shown. With *single* strand of orange, aqua, or green as desired, embroider randomly placed eight-pointed stars in different sizes on public side of collar by working two cross-stitches one above the other.

Button Embellishment

Sew a larger decorative white button to center back about 3 (3½, 4)" (7.5 [9, 10] cm) down from collar seam. Sew 4 smaller white buttons about ¾" (2 cm) away from button at center back, directly above, below, and to each side of center button. With double strand of aqua, work a diamond with 1" (2.5 cm) straight sts around center button. Sew 4 randomly placed small white buttons to each front, then with a double strand of orange, aqua, or green, as desired work a diamond with ¾" (2 cm) straight sts around each button. Sew rem buttons to garter st edging around bottom edges of body and sleeves.

PATCHWORK JACKET
GAYLE BUNN

Gayle Bunn took inspiration from old quilts made from square blocks of bright fabrics that had faded over time for the patchwork squares in this cropped jacket. "I love vintage textiles and this patchwork is meant to suggest old herringbone tweed mixed with checks and classic argyles for a knitterly touch," explains Gayle. The cropped and curvy shape is a fresh take on women's Spencer jackets of the early nineteenth century. The color work is achieved through a combination of Fair Isle and intarsia techniques.

NOTES

❖ Work the Patchwork chart in stockinette-stitch intarsia, using separate lengths of yarn for each color section and twisting yarns together between blocks to avoid leaving holes. In adjacent blocks of the diagonal and grid patterns, the red and green yarns can be stranded all the way across both blocks to reduce the number of ends to weave in. The tan and teal background colors for these blocks can be worked with a separate strand of yarn for each block. For the argyle blocks, use separate lengths of yarn for the center diamond and the red background on each side; do not strand the red across the back of the large diamond and do not strand the argyle yarns across the back of any other blocks.

❖ If desired, the single dark brown stitches of the argyle Xs and center dots in the grid pattern of the Patchwork chart may be worked in the background color and embroidered in duplicate stitch (see page 149) after the knitting is finished, using the chart as a guide.

BACK

With red and larger needles, CO 89 (93, 103, 109) sts. Beg and ending where indicated for your size, work Rows 1–52 of Patchwork chart (see Notes)—piece measures about 9" (23 cm) from CO. Note: Garter stitch lower edging will add about ½" (1.3 cm) more to this length when applied during finishing.

Shape Armholes

Cont as charted, BO 7 (8, 9, 10) sts at beg of next 2 rows—75 (77, 85, 89) sts rem. Dec 1 st each end of needle every RS row 7 (7, 9, 10) times—61 (63, 67, 69) sts rem. Work even until Row 94 (96, 98, 100) of chart has been completed—armholes measure about 7¼ (7½, 8, 8½)" (18.5 [19, 20.5, 21.5] cm).

FINISHED SIZE

34½ (36¼, 39½, 42¼)" (87.5 [92, 100.5, 107.5] cm) bust circumference, buttoned. Jacket shown measures 34½" (87.5 cm).

YARN

Worsted weight (#4 Medium).

Shown here: Mission Falls 1824 Wool (100% superwash merino wool; 85 yd [78 m]/50 g): #534 rhubarb (red), 4 (4, 5, 5) balls; #002 stone (tan), 2 (2, 2, 3) balls; #028 pistachio (green), 3 (3, 4, 4) balls; #030 teal, 4 (5, 6, 7) balls; #008 earth (dark brown), 1 ball for all sizes.

NEEDLES

Body—size 8 (5 mm). Edging—size 7 (4.5 mm): 32" (80 cm) circular (cir). Adjust needle size if necessary to obtain the correct gauge.

NOTIONS

Stitch holder; markers (m); tapestry needle; two ¾" (2 cm) buttons (button shown here is style #B12 from Mission Falls).

GAUGE

21 stitches and 23 rows = 4" (10 cm) in stockinette-stitch intarsia from Patchwork chart, worked on larger needles; 21 stitches and 20 rows = 4" (10 cm) in stockinette color-work pattern from Right Sleeve and Left Sleeve charts, worked on larger needles.

Shape Shoulders

Cont as charted, BO 7 (7, 8, 8) sts at beg of next 2 rows, then BO 8 (8, 9, 9) sts at beg of foll 2 rows—31 (33, 33, 35) sts rem. Place sts on holder.

LEFT FRONT

With red and larger needles, CO 26 (28, 33, 36) sts. Beg and ending where indicated for your size, work Row 1 of Patchwork chart. Beg with Row 2, inc 1 st at center front edge (beg of WS rows; end of RS rows) every row 18 times, then every other row 2 times—46 (48, 53, 56) sts. Work even until Row 40 of chart has been completed—piece measures about 7" (18 cm) from CO.

Shape Neck and Armhole

Note: Armhole shaping begins while neck shaping is still in progress; read the next sections all the way through before proceeding so you do not accidentally work past the point where the armhole begins. Beg with Row 41 of chart, dec 1 st at center front edge (end of RS rows) every other row 7 (8, 7, 8) times, then every 4th row 10 (10, 11, 11) times—17 (18, 18, 19) sts total removed at neck edge. *At the same time,* after Row 52 has been completed, shape armhole as for back by binding off 7 (8, 9, 10) sts at beg of Row 53, then dec 1 st at armhole edge at beg of next 7 (7, 9, 10) RS rows—14 (15, 18, 20) sts total removed at armhole edge. Cont even until Row 94 (96, 98, 100) of chart has been completed—when all neck and armhole shaping has been completed, 15 (15, 17, 17) sts rem; armhole measures about 7¼ (7½, 8, 8½)" (18.5 [19, 20.5, 21.5] cm).

Shape Shoulder

Cont as charted, BO 7 (7, 8, 8) sts beg of next RS row, then BO rem 8 (8, 9, 9) sts at beg of foll RS row.

▪ red; k on RS, p on WS	⬛ dark brown; k on RS, p on WS, or embroider with duplicate st
· tan; k on RS, p on WS	
− green; k on RS, p on WS	☐ pattern repeat
+ teal; k on RS, p on WS	

―― size 34½"
―― size 36½"
―― size 39½"
―― size 42¼"

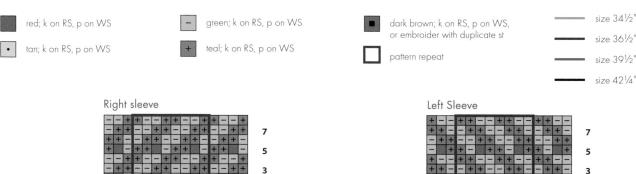

Right sleeve

7
5
3
1

end 39½" 42¼" end 34½" 36½" beg 34½" 36½" beg 39½" 42¼"

Left Sleeve

7
5
3
1

end 39½" 42¼" end 34½" 36½" beg 34½" 36½" beg 39½" 42¼"

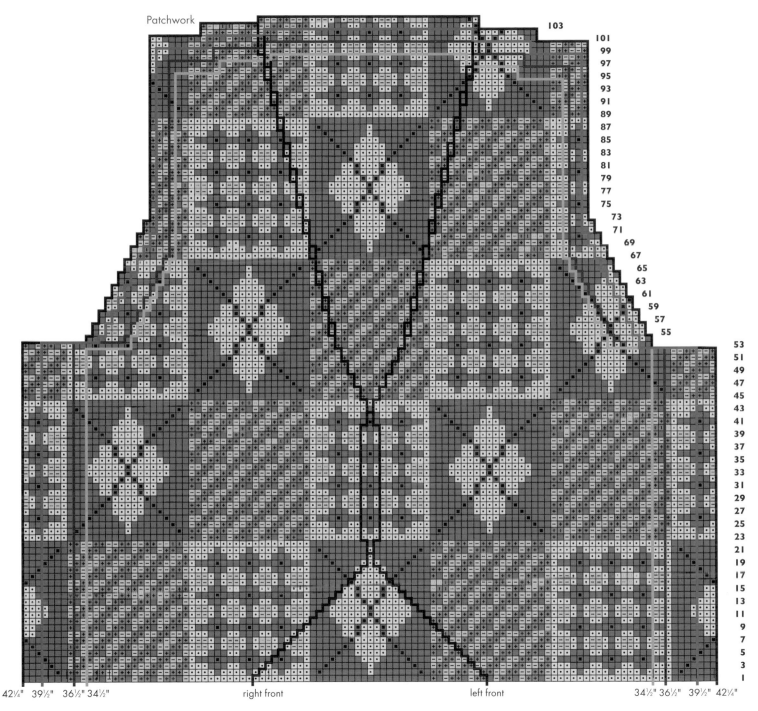

Patchwork

103
101
99
97
95
93
91
89
87
85
83
81
79
77
75
73
71
69
67
65
63
61
59
57
55

53
51
49
47
45
43
41
39
37
35
33
31
29
27
25
23
21
19
17
15
13
11
9
7
5
3
1

42¼" 39½" 36½" 34½"   right front   left front   34½" 36½" 39½" 42¼"

RIGHT FRONT

With red and larger needles, CO 26 (28, 33, 36) sts. Beg and ending where indicated for your size, work Row 1 of Patchwork chart. Beg with Row 2, inc 1 st at center front edge (end of WS rows; beg of RS rows) every row 18 times, then every other row 2 times—46 (48, 53, 56) sts. Work even until Row 40 of chart has been completed—piece measures about 7" (18 cm) from CO.

Shape Neck and Armhole

Note: Armhole shaping begins while neck shaping is still in progress; read the next sections all the way through before proceeding so you do not accidentally work past the point where the armhole begins. Beg with Row 41 of chart, dec 1 st at center front edge (beg of RS rows) every other row 7 (8, 7, 8) times, then every 4th row 10 (10, 11, 11) times—17 (18, 18, 19) sts total removed at neck edge. *At the same time,* after Row 53 has been completed, shape armhole as for back by binding off 7 (8, 9, 10) sts at beg of Row 54, then dec 1 st at armhole edge at end of next 7 (7, 9, 10) RS rows—14 (15, 18, 20) sts total removed at armhole edge. Cont even until Row 95 (97, 99, 101) of chart has been completed—when all neck and armhole shaping has been completed, 15 (15, 17, 17) sts rem; armhole measures about 7¼ (7½, 8, 8½)" (18.5 [19, 20.5, 21.5] cm).

Shape Shoulder

Cont as charted, BO 7 (7, 8, 8) sts beg of next WS row, then BO rem 8 (8, 9, 9) sts at beg of foll WS row.

RIGHT SLEEVE

With teal and larger needles, CO 62 sts for all sizes.
Row 1: (RS): *K2, p2; rep from * to last 2 sts, k2.
Row 2: *P2, k2; rep from * to last 2 sts, p2.

Embrace swatch knitting. When you know your gauge you can knit *anything.*

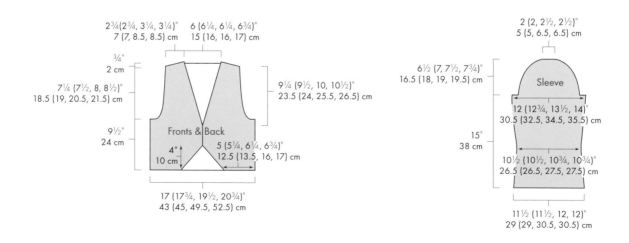

2¾ (2¾, 3¼, 3¼)"
7 (7, 8.5, 8.5) cm

6 (6¼, 6¼, 6¾)"
15 (16, 16, 17) cm

¾"
2 cm

7¼ (7½, 8, 8½)"
18.5 (19, 20.5, 21.5) cm

9¼ (9½, 10, 10½)"
23.5 (24, 25.5, 26.5) cm

9½"
24 cm

Fronts & Back

4"
10 cm

5 (5¼, 6¼, 6¾)"
12.5 (13.5, 16, 17) cm

17 (17¾, 19½, 20¾)"
43 (45, 49.5, 52.5) cm

2 (2, 2½, 2½)"
5 (5, 6.5, 6.5) cm

6½ (7, 7½, 7¾)"
16.5 (18, 19, 19.5) cm

Sleeve

12 (12¾, 13½, 14)"
30.5 (32.5, 34.5, 35.5) cm

15"
38 cm

10½ (10½, 10¾, 10¾)"
26.5 (26.5, 27.5, 27.5) cm

11½ (11½, 12, 12)"
29 (29, 30.5, 30.5) cm

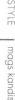

Rep these 2 rows once more, and *at the same time* dec 1 (dec 1, inc 1, inc 1) st in center of last row—61 (61, 63, 63) sts. Beg and ending where indicated for your size, work Row 1 of Right Sleeve chart. Cont in patt from chart, work Rows 2–8. Dec 1 st each end of next RS row (Row 1 of chart), then every foll 10th row 2 more times—55 (55, 57, 57) sts rem; piece measures about 6½" (16.5 cm) from CO. Work 9 (9, 5, 9) rows even in patt—piece measures about 8¼ (8¼, 7½, 8¼)" (21 [21, 19, 21] cm) from CO. Inc 1 st end of needle on next row, then every foll 8th (6th, 6th, 4th) row 3 (5, 6, 7) more times, working new sts into patt—63 (67, 71, 73) sts. Cont even in patt until piece measures 15" (38 cm) from CO for all sizes, ending with a WS row.

Shape Cap

Cont in patt, BO 3 (4, 4, 4) sts at beg of next 2 rows—57 (59, 63, 65) sts rem. Dec 1 st at each end of needle on next 8 (9, 10, 11) RS rows—41 (41, 43, 43) sts rem. Dec 1 st at each end of needle *every row* 15 times—11 (11, 13, 13) times. BO all sts.

LEFT SLEEVE

Work as for right sleeve, substituting Left Sleeve chart.

FINISHING

Block pieces to measurements. If you did not knit the dark brown sts of the Patchwork chart (see Notes), add them using dark brown threaded on a tapestry needle in duplicate stitch (see page 149). With yarn threaded on a tapestry needle, sew fronts to back at shoulders. Sew side seams.

Edging

With teal, cir needle, RS facing, and beg at right side seam, pick up and knit 22 (24, 29, 32) sts across CO edge of right front, 17 sts along shaped edge, pm to indicate buttonhole position, pick up and knit 13 sts along straight selvedge, 49 (51, 53, 55) sts along right V-neck to shoulder seam, k31 (33, 33, 35) held back neck sts dec 2 sts evenly across as you work them, pick up and knit 49 (51, 53, 55) sts along left front V-neck, 13 sts along straight selvedge, 17 sts along shaped edge, 22 (24, 29, 32) sts across CO edge of left front, and 80 (84, 93, 99) sts across CO edge of back—311 (325, 348, 366) sts total. Pm and join for working in the rnd. *Next rnd:* *Purl to buttonhole marker, p1, BO 2 sts, p8, BO 2 sts, purl to end. *Next rnd:* Knit, using the backward-loop method (see Glossary, page 152) to CO 2 sts over BO gap in previous rnd to complete buttonholes. BO all sts pwise.

With yarn threaded on a tapestry needle, sew sleeve seams. Sew sleeve caps into armholes. Weave in loose ends. With WS facing, lightly steam-press seams and edging. Sew buttons to left front opposite buttonholes.

MODERN QUILT WRAP
MAGS KANDIS

What could be more comforting than being wrapped up in the warmth of a colorful quilt? Very loosely based on the traditional Log Cabin quilt block, **Mags Kandis** worked this wrap/oversized scarf square by square in the easy and satisfying mitered-square method of color knitting. This is as effortless as working in stripes, but the results are far more impressive. As this project is worked one color as a time, it's perfect for thinking about and playing with color.

STITCH GUIDE

Small Square (worked on 24 sts).
Row 1: (WS) K12, place marker (pm), k12.
Even-numbered Rows 2–20: (RS) Knit to 2 sts before m, k2tog, slip marker (sl m), k2tog through back loops (tbl), knit to end—2 sts dec'd; 4 sts rem after completing Row 20.
Odd-numbered Rows 3–21: Knit.
Row 22: K2tog, k2tog tbl—2 sts rem.
Use left needle tip to lift second st on right needle over the first as if to BO—1 st. Cut yarn, draw tail through rem st, and pull tight to fasten off.

Large Square (worked on 48 sts):
Row 1: (WS) K24, pm, k24.
Even-numbered Rows 2–44: (RS) Knit to 2 sts before m, k2tog, sl m, k2tog tbl, knit to end—2 sts dec'd; 4 sts rem after completing Row 44.
Odd-numbered Rows 3–45: Knit.
Row 46: K2tog, k2tog tbl—2 sts rem.
Use left needle tip to lift second st on right needle over the first as if to BO—1 st. Cut yarn, draw tail through rem st, and pull tight to fasten off.

NOTE
❖ Refer to the diagram on page 27 for working order and placement of blocks.

FINISHED SIZE
About 16½" (42 cm) wide and 66" (168 cm) long, after blocking.

YARN
Sportweight (#2 Fine).

Shown here: Rowan Kidsilk Haze (70% super kid mohair; 30% silk; 230 yd [210 m]/25 g): #597 jelly (lime green; A), #596 marmalade (orange, B), #583 blushes (rose; C), #600 dewberry (lavender; D), #582 trance (medium blue; E), #578 swish (gold; F), #581 meadow (pale blue; G), #595 liqueur (dark red; H), and #588 drab (grey; I), 1 ball each

NEEDLES
Size 7 (4.5 mm). *Note:* a 16" (40 cm) bamboo circular needle is recommended. Adjust needle size if necessary to obtain the correct gauge.

NOTIONS
Marker (m); tapestry needle.

GAUGE
Small square measures 2¾" (7 cm) square; large square measures 5½" (14 cm) square, both after blocking.

FIRST HALF

Block 1

With A, CO 24 sts. Work Small Square (see Stitch Guide), working Rows 1–9 with A and Rows 10–22 with B.

Block 2

With I, CO 12 sts, then pick up and knit 12 sts evenly spaced along side edge of Block 1 as shown in diagram at right—24 sts. Work Small Square, working Rows 1–5 with I, Rows 6–15 with D, and Rows 16–22 with F.

Block 3

With F, pick up and knit 12 sts evenly spaced across top of Block 1, then use the backward-loop method (see Glossary, page 152) to CO 12 sts—24 sts total. Work Small Square, working Rows 1–5 with F, Rows 6–13 with E, and Rows 14–22 with H.

Block 4

With C, pick up and knit 12 sts evenly spaced across top of Block 2, then 12 sts evenly spaced along right side of Block 3—24 sts total. Work Small Square, working Rows 1–3 with C, Rows 4–9 with I, and Rows 12–22 with A.

Block 5

With G, CO 24 sts, then pick up and knit 24 sts evenly spaced along right sides of Blocks 2 and 4—48 sts total. Work Large Square (see Stitch Guide), working Rows 1–9 with G, Rows 10–17 with H, Rows 18–23 with C, Rows 24–33 with A, and Rows 34–46 with F.

Block 6

With D, CO 24 sts, then pick up and knit 24 sts evenly spaced along right side of Block 5—48 sts total. Work Large Square, working Rows 1–5 with D, Rows 6–15 with B, Rows 16–23 with E, Rows 24–31 with F, and Rows 32–46 with C.

Block 7

With H, CO 24 sts, then pick up and knit 24 sts evenly spaced across top of Block 6—48 sts total. Work Large Square, working Rows 1–9 with H, Rows 10–19 with D, Rows 20–27 with A, Rows 28–33 with G, and Rows 34–46 with B.

Block 8

With E, pick up and knit 12 sts evenly spaced along lower half of left side of Block 7, then pick up and knit 12 sts evenly spaced across first half of top edge of Block 5—24 sts total. Work Small Square, working Rows 1–9 with E and Rows 10–22 with C.

Block 9

With I, pick up and knit 12 sts evenly spaced along left side of Block 8, then pick up and knit 12 sts evenly spaced across second half of top edge of Block 5—24 sts total. Work Small Square, working Rows 1–5 with I, Rows 6–11 with B, and Rows 12–22 with D.

First Half

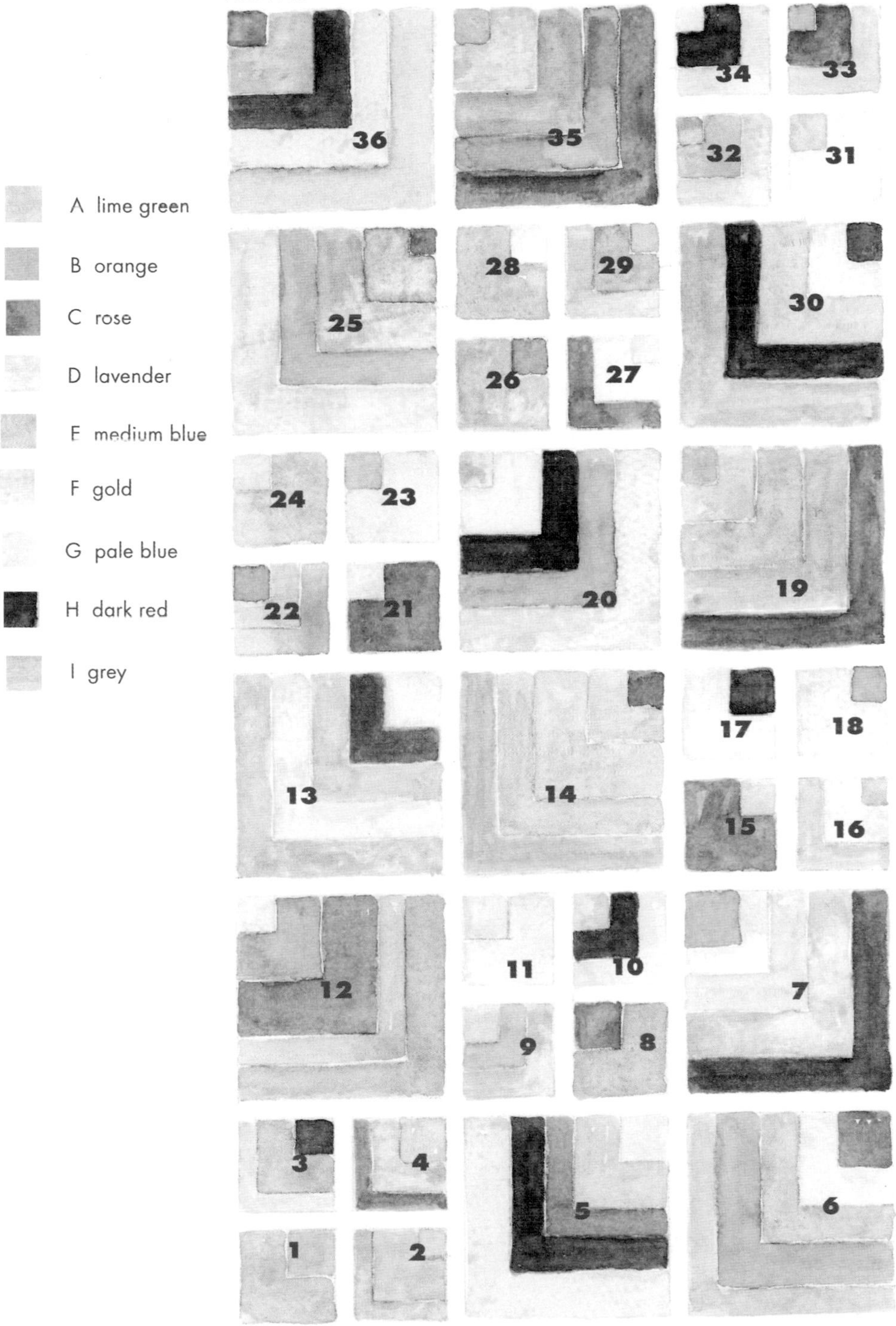

A lime green
B orange
C rose
D lavender
E medium blue
F gold
G pale blue
H dark red
I grey
36
35
34
33
32
31
25
28
29
30
26
27
24
23
20
19
22
21
13
14
17
18
15
16
12
11
10
7
9
8
3
4
5
6
1
2

Block 10

With F, pick up and knit 12 sts evenly spaced along top half of left side of Block 7, then pick up and knit 12 sts evenly spaced along top edge of Block 8—24 sts total. Work Small Square, working Rows 1–5 with F, Rows 6–11 with H, and Rows 12–22 with D.

Block 11

With G, pick up and knit 12 sts evenly spaced along left side of Block 10, then pick up and knit 12 sts evenly spaced along top edge of Block 9—24 sts total. Work Small Square, working Rows 1–9 with G and Rows 10–22 with F.

Block 12

With E, pick up and knit 24 sts evenly spaced along left sides of Blocks 11 and 9, then pick up and knit 24 sts evenly spaced along top edges of Blocks 4 and 3—48 sts total. Work Large Square, working Rows 1–7 with E, Rows 8–13 with A, Rows 14–25 with C, Rows 26–35 with B, and Rows 36–46 with G.

Block 13

With I, pick up and knit 24 st evenly spaced along top edge of Block 12, then use the backward-loop method to CO 24 sts—48 sts total. Work Large Square, working Rows 1–9 with I, Rows 10–17 with F, Rows 18–25 with D, Rows 26–33 with H, and Rows 34–46 with G.

Block 14

With B, pick up and knit 24 sts evenly spaced along top edges of Blocks 10 and 11, then pick up and knit 24 sts evenly spaced along right side of Block 13—48 sts total. Work Large Square, working Rows 1–7 with B, Rows 8–15 with E, Rows 16–27 with A, Rows 28–35 with D, and Rows 36–46 with C.

Block 15

With C, pick up and knit 12 sts evenly spaced along second half of top edge of Block 7, then pick up and knit 12 sts evenly spaced along lower half of right side of Block 14—24 sts total. Work Small Square, working Rows 1–11 with C and Rows 12–22 with A.

Block 16

With I, pick up and knit 12 sts evenly spaced along first half of top edge of Block 7, then pick up and knit 12 sts evenly spaced along right side of Block 15—24 sts total. Work Small Square, working Rows 1–5 with I, Rows 6–13 with F, and Rows 14–22 with E.

Block 17

With F, pick up and knit 12 sts evenly spaced along top edge of Block 15, then pick up and knit 12 sts evenly spaced along top half of right side of Block 14—24 sts total. Work Small Square, working Rows 1–9 with F and Rows 10–22 with H.

Block 18

With G, pick up and knit 12 sts evenly spaced across top edge of Block 16, then pick up and knit 12 sts evenly spaced along right side of Block 17—24 sts total. Work Small Square, working Rows 1–11 with G and Rows 12–22 with B.

Block 19

With C, use the backward-loop method to CO 24 sts, then pick up and knit 24 sts evenly spaced across top edges of Blocks 18 and 17—48 sts total. Work Large Square, working Rows 1–7 with C, Rows 8–17 with I, Rows 18–27 with E, Rows 28–35 with A, and Rows 36–46 with B.

Block 20

With D, pick up and knit 24 sts evenly spaced along right side of Block 19, then pick up and knit 24 sts evenly spaced across top edge of Block 14—48 sts total. Work Large Square, working Rows 1–9 with D, Rows 10–17 with B, Rows 18–25 with H, Rows 26–35 with F, and Rows 36–46 with I.

Block 21

With C, pick up and knit 12 sts evenly spaced along lower half of left side of Block 20, then pick up and knit 12 sts evenly spaced across first half of top edge of Block 13—24 sts total. Work Small Square, working Rows 1–11 with C and Rows 12–22 with F.

Block 22

With A, pick up and knit 12 sts evenly spaced along left side of Block 21, then pick up and knit 12 sts evenly spaced across second half of top edge of Block 13—24 sts total. Work Small Square, working Rows 1–5 with A, Rows 6–11 with D, and Rows 12–22 with B.

Block 23

With G, pick up and knit 12 sts evenly spaced along top half of left side of Block 20, then pick up and knit 12 sts evenly spaced across top edge of Block 21—24 sts total. Work Small Square, working Rows 1–11 with G and Rows 12–22 with D.

Block 24

With E, pick up and knit 12 sts evenly spaced along left side of Block 23, then pick up and knit 12 sts evenly spaced across top edge of Block 22—24 sts total. Work Small Square, working Rows 1–11 with E and Rows 12–22 with A.

Block 25

With F, pick up and knit 24 sts evenly spaced across top edges of Blocks 23 and 24, then use the backward-loop method to CO 24 sts—48 sts total. Work Large Square, working Rows 1–9 with F, Rows 10–17 with B, Rows 18–27 with I, Rows 28–37 with E, and Rows 38–46 with C.

Block 26

With E, pick up and knit 12 sts evenly spaced across second half of top edge of Block 20, then pick up and knit 12 sts evenly spaced along lower half of right side of Block 25—24 sts total. Work Small Square, working Rows 1–11 with E and Rows 12–22 with B.

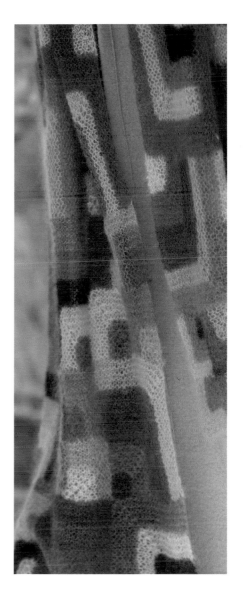

If you're new to creating your own designs, begin with a project that doesn't have to fit.

Block 27

With C, pick up and knit 12 sts evenly spaced across first half of top edge of Block 20, then pick up and knit 12 sts evenly spaced along right side of Block 26—24 sts total. Work Small Square, working Rows 1–5 with C, Rows 6–13 with G, and Rows 14–22 with F.

Block 28

With A, pick up and knit 12 sts evenly spaced across top edge of Block 26, then pick up and knit 12 sts evenly spaced along top half of right side of Block 25—24 sts total. Work Small Square, working Rows 1–11 with A and Rows 12–22 with G.

Block 29

With D, pick up and knit 12 sts evenly spaced across top edge of Block 27, then pick up and knit 12 sts evenly spaced along right side of Block 28—24 sts total. Work Small Square, working Rows 1–5 with D, Rows 6–13 with E, and Rows 14–22 with A.

Block 30

With I, pick up and knit 24 sts evenly spaced across top edge of Block 19, then pick up and knit 24 sts evenly spaced along right sides of Blocks 27 and 29—48 sts total. Work Large Square, working Rows 1–9 with I, Rows 10–17 with H, Rows 18–27 with A, Rows 28–35 with F, and Rows 36–46 with C.

Block 31

With G, CO 12 sts, then pick up and knit 12 sts evenly spaced across first half of top edge of Block 30—24 sts total. Work Small Square, working Rows 1–11 with G and Rows 12–22 with E.

Block 32

With D, pick up and knit 12 sts evenly spaced along left side of Block 31, then pick up and knit 12 sts evenly spaced across second half of top edge of Block 30—24 sts total. Work Small Square, working Rows 1–5 with D, Rows 6–13 with A, and Rows 14–22 with I.

Block 33

With A, CO 12 sts, then pick up and knit 12 sts evenly spaced across top edge of Block 31— 24 sts total. Work Small Square, working Rows 1–5 with A, Rows 6–13 with C, and Rows 14–22 with B.

Block 34

With F, pick up and knit 12 sts evenly spaced along left side of Block 33, then pick up and knit 12 sts evenly spaced across top edge of Block 32—24 sts total. Work Small Square, working Rows 1–5 with F, Rows 6–11 with H, and Rows 12–22 with G.

Block 35

With C, pick up and knit 24 sts along left sides of Blocks 34 and 32, then pick up and knit 24 sts evenly spaced across top edges of Blocks 29 and 28—48 sts total. Work Large Square, working Rows 1–7 with C, Rows 8–15 with B, Rows 16–25 with I, Rows 26–35 with D, and Rows 36–46 with A.

Block 36

With D, pick up and knit 24 sts evenly spaced along left side of Block 35, then pick up and knit 24 sts evenly spaced across top edge of Block 25—48 sts total. Work Large Square, working Rows 1–9 with D, Rows 10–17 with G, Rows 18–25 with H, Rows 26–35 with E, and Rows 36–46 with C.

This completes first half of wrap.

SECOND HALF

Work the first group of blocks for the second half directly onto the top edge of the first half, modifying the block instructions for the first half as foll:

Block 1

With A, pick up and knit 12 sts evenly spaced across second half of top edge of Block 36, then CO 12 sts—24 sts. Work as for Block 1 in first half.

Block 2

With I, pick up and knit 12 sts evenly spaced across first half of top edge of Block 36, then pick up and knit 12 sts evenly spaced along right side of Block 1—24 sts. Work as for Block 2 in first half.

Blocks 3 and 4

Work as for first half.

Block 5

With G, pick up and knit 24 sts evenly spaced across top edge of Block 35, then pick up and knit 24 sts evenly spaced along right sides of Blocks 2 and 4—48 sts total. Work as for Block 5 in first half.

Block 6

With D, pick up and knit 24 sts evenly spaced across top edge of Blocks 33 and 34, then pick up and knit 24 sts along right side of Block 5—48 sts total. Work as for Block 6 in first half.

Blocks 7–36

Work as for first half.

FINISHING

Weave in loose ends. Block lightly to measurements.

CHILD'S TIBETAN JACKET
TARA JON MANNING

Styled after the traditional wool coats of the high Himalayan region, **Tara Jon Manning's** child's jacket features the boxy shape, colorful trim, and stand-up collar immediately recognizable as distinctive folk elements of Tibetan and Nepalese outerwear. Worked here in traditional colors, this garment features the added flourish of playful embroidered embellishment, referencing the rich brocades of Tibetan shrines and sacred regalia.

> **NOTES**
> ❖ Kids don't come in standard sizes. Measure a favorite or slightly oversized piece of the child's clothing for a reference when selecting which size to knit. Plan on purchasing an extra ball of the main color if you make the body or sleeves longer than suggested here. If lengthening the body, add extra rows to the body above the lower border but below the armhole shaping. For longer sleeves, work extra rows after completing the sleeve shaping, but before working the cuff border.
>
> ❖ Work the multicolor rows of the borders in stockinette-stitch intarsia, using separate lengths of yarn for each color section, and twisting yarns together at color changes to avoid leaving holes. Do not strand the unused colors across the back side of the work.

BACK

With MC, loosely CO 54 (57, 60) sts.

Row 1: (RS) With MC, purl.

Row 2: With MC, knit.

Row 3: Set up colors for working intarsia blocks (see Notes) as foll: *K3 with green, k3 with blue, k3 with gold, k3 with MC; rep from * to last 6 (9, 0) sts, end k3 (3, 0) with green, k3 (3, 0) with blue, k0 (3, 0) with gold.

Rows 4 and 5: Work in St st, working each 3-st group with its established color.

Rows 6 and 7: With gold, purl all sts.

Row 8: With gold, knit.

Cont with MC, work even in St st until piece measures 6½ (6½, 7)" (16.5 [16.5, 18] cm) from CO, ending with a WS row.

Shape Armholes

BO 2 sts at beg of next 2 rows—50 (53, 56) sts rem. Cont even in St st until armholes measure 5¾ (6½, 7)" (14.5 [16.5, 18] cm), ending with a WS row.

FINISHED SIZE
25½ (27, 28½)" (65 [68.5, 72.5] cm) chest circumference. To fit size 2 (4, 6/8) years. Jacket shown measures 28½" (72.5 cm).

YARN
Worsted weight (#4 Medium).
Shown here: Mission Falls 1824 Cotton (100% cotton; 84 yd [77 m] /50 g): #207 chili (MC, rust), 5 (6, 6) skeins; #204 lentil (gold), #301 fennel (green), and #401 chicory (blue), 1 skein each.

NEEDLES
Size 8 (5 mm). Adjust needle size if necessary to obtain the correct gauge.

NOTIONS
Stitch holders; spare needle same size as main needles for three-needle bind-off; tapestry needle; tailor's chalk (available at fabric stores); five 1½" (3.8) toggle buttons; size J/10 (6 mm) crochet hook.

GAUGE
17 stitches and 25 rows = 4" (10 cm) in stockinette stitch.

Shape Neck

K14 (14, 15), BO center 22 (25, 26) sts, knit to end—14 (14, 15) sts rem each side. Place sts on separate holders.

LEFT FRONT

With MC, loosely CO 27 (30, 30) sts.

Rows 1 and 2: Work as for back.

Row 3: (RS) Set up colors for working intarsia blocks as foll: *K3 with green, k3 with blue, k3 with gold, k3 with MC; rep from * to last 3 (6, 6) sts, end k3 with green, k0 (3, 3) with blue.

Rows 4–8: Work as for back border.

Cont with MC, work even in St st until piece measures 6½ (6½, 7)" (16.5 [16.5, 18] cm) from CO, ending with a WS row.

Shape Armhole

BO 2 sts at beg of next RS row—25 (28, 28) sts rem. Cont even in St st until armhole measures 3¼ (3¾, 4)" (8.5 [9.5, 10] cm), ending with a RS row.

Shape Neck

BO 5 (7, 6) sts at beg of next WS row, purl to end—20 (21, 22) sts rem. Dec 1 st at neck edge (end of RS rows) every RS row 6 (7, 7) times—14 (14, 15) sts rem. Cont even until armhole measures 5¾ (6½, 7)" (14.5 [16.5, 18] cm), ending with a WS row. Place sts on holder.

Add embroidery to give a special "handmade" feel to a garment.

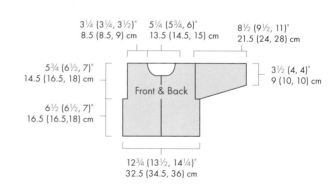

RIGHT FRONT

With MC, loosely CO 27 (30, 30) sts.

Rows 1 and 2: Work as for back.

Row 3: (RS) Set up colors for working in-tarsia blocks as foll: *K3 with gold, k3 with MC, k3 with green, k3 with blue; rep from * to last 3 (6, 6) sts, end k3 with gold, k0 (3, 3) with MC.

Rows 4–8: Work as for back border. Cont with MC, work even in St st until piece measures 6½ (6½, 7)" (16.5 [16.5, 18] cm) from CO, ending with a RS row.

Shape Armhole

BO 2 sts at beg of next WS row—25 (28, 28) sts rem. Cont even in St st until armhole measures 3¼ (3¾, 4)" (8.5 [9.5, 10] cm), ending with a WS row.

Shape Neck

BO 5 (7, 6) sts at beg of next RS row, knit to end—20 (21, 22) sts rem. Dec 1 st at neck edge (beg of RS rows) every RS row 6 (7, 7) times—14 (14, 15) sts rem. Cont even until armhole measures 5¾ (6½, 7)" (14.5 [16.5, 18] cm), ending with a WS row. Place sts on holder.

JOIN SHOULDERS

Place held sts for left front and left back shoulder on separate needles. Hold pieces tog with RS touching and WS of garment facing out. Use the spare needle and the three-needle bind-off method (see Glossary, page 152) to join left shoulder sts tog. Join right shoulder sts in the same manner.

SLEEVES

With MC and RS facing, pick up and knit 50 (56, 60) sts evenly spaced bet armhole notches, picking up the first and last sts in the corners of the notches. Work in St st, and *at the same time* dec 1 st each end of needle every 4 rows 9 (11, 13) times—32 (34, 34) sts rem. Cont even until sleeve measures 7¼ (8¼, 9¾)" (18.5 [21, 25] cm) from pick-up row, ending with a RS row. With gold, purl 1 WS row, dec 2 (1, 1) st(s) evenly spaced—30 (33, 33) sts rem. Work cuff border as foll:

Row 1: (RS) With gold, purl.

Row 2: With gold, knit.

Row 3: Set up colors for working intarsia blocks as foll: *K3 with green, k3 with MC, k3 with gold, k3 with blue; rep from * to last 6 (9, 9) sts, end k3 with green, k3 with MC, k0 (3, 3) with gold.

Rows 4 and 5: Work in St st, working each 3-st group in its established color.

Rows 6 and 7: With MC, purl.

Row 8: With MC, knit—sleeve measures about 8½ (9½, 11)" (21.5 [24, 28] cm) from pick-up row.

Loosely BO all sts, leaving a long tail for sewing seams.

FINISHING

Block pieces to measurements.

Front Bands

With gold and RS facing, pick up and knit 45 (48, 54) sts evenly spaced along left front edge.

Row 1: (WS) With gold, knit.

Row 2: With gold, purl.

Row 3: Set up colors for working intarsia

blocks as foll: *P3 with MC, p3 with gold, p3 with blue, p3 with green; rep from * to last 9 (0, 6) sts, end p3 (0, 3) with MC, p3 (0, 3) with gold, p3 (0, 0) with blue.

Rows 4 and 5: Work in St st, working each 3-st group in its established color.

Rows 6–8: With MC, knit.

Loosely BO all sts. With gold and RS facing, pick up and knit 45 (48, 54) sts evenly spaced along right front edge.

Rows 1 and 2: Work as for left front band.

Row 3: Set up colors for working intarsia blocks as foll: *P3 with gold, p3 with MC, p3 with green, p3 with blue; rep from * to last 9 (0, 6) sts, end p3 (0, 3) with gold, p3 (0, 3) with MC, p3 (0, 0) with green.

Rows 4–8: Work as for left front band.

Loosely BO all sts.

Neckband

With gold and RS facing, pick up and knit 63 (69, 75) sts evenly around neck edge as foll: 20 (22, 24) sts along right front edge, 23 (25, 27) sts along back neck, and 20 (22, 24) sts along left front edge.

Row 1: (WS) With gold, knit.

Row 2: With gold, purl.

Row 3: Set up colors for working intarsia blocks as foll: *P3 with gold, p3 with MC, p3 with green, p3 with blue; rep from * to last 3 (9, 3) sts, end p3 with gold, p0 (3, 0) with MC, p0 (3, 0) with green.

Rows 4 and 5: Work in St st, working each 3-st group in its established color.

Rows 6–8: With MC, knit.

Loosely BO all sts.

Buttons and Button Loops

Sew 5 buttons evenly spaced along left front for girls or right front for boys, with the highest and lowest buttons centered on a gold reverse St st ridge. With MC and crochet hook, make 5 crochet chains (see Glossary, page 154), each about 3" (7.5 cm) long for button loops. Fold each chain in half to form a loop and with MC threaded on a tapestry needle, sew a loop to the opposite front edge to correspond to each button position.

Embroidery

With chalk and using templates as a guide, draw random freehand spirals and S-shaped curlicues in different sizes on fronts, back, and sleeves as shown in photographs. With gold threaded on a tapestry needle, work chain-stitch embroidery (see page 148) along chalk lines. Weave in loose ends. With MC tails from sleeves threaded on a tapestry needle, sew sleeve and side seams.

Di Gilpin creates an "If it's Tuesday, it must be Belgium" whirlwind tour of Europe with this bolero vest. The shape is drawn from a traditional Greek waistcoat, and the motifs come from the Chateau de Montresor in the Loire Valley, France. Reports Di, "The ancient wallpapers escaped the destruction of the revolution and show the amazing skills of the French wallpaper makers! I allowed the design to develop into the style of Jujol, the Spanish architect who worked with Gaudi, and whose house contained decorations handpainted in this style."

NOTES

❖ The waistcoat is worked in one piece to the armholes, then divided for working the fronts and back separately.

❖ Work the charts in stockinette-stitch intarsia, using separate balls or bobbins of yarn for each color section and twisting yarns together at color changes to avoid leaving holes. Do not strand the unused color across the back side of the work.

LOWER BODY

With MC and longer smaller-size needle, CO 175 (181, 187) sts. Do not join. Work back and forth in rows as foll:

Row 1: (RS) Knit every st through back loop (tbl).

Row 2: *K2tog, yo; rep from * to last st, k1.

Row 3: Knit.

Rows 4 and 5: Rep Rows 2 and 3.

Size 39" only: Work Row 2 once more, inc 1 st by working M1 (see Glossary, page 155) before final k1 at end of row—176 sts; 6 rows completed; edging measures about 1" (2.5 cm) from CO.

Sizes 40½ (41¾)" only: Rep Rows 2 and 3 two times, then work Row 2 once more, inc 1 st by working M1 (see Glossary, page 155) before final k1 at end of row—182 (188) sts; 10 rows completed; edging measures about 1½" (3.8 cm) from CO.

FINISHED SIZE
39 (40½, 41¾)" (99 [103, 106] cm) chest/bust circumference. Waistcoat shown measures 39" (99 cm).

YARN
Worsted weight (#4 Medium).

Shown here: The Fibre Company Terra (60% merino, 20% baby alpaca, 20% silk; 100 yd [91 m]/50 g): henna (dark reddish brown; MC), 4 (5, 6) skeins, black walnut (dark green; CC), 1 skein for all sizes.

NEEDLES
Front and back—size 9 (5.5 mm): 32" (80 cm) circular (cir). Edging—size 8 (5 mm): 20" and 32" (50 and 80 cm) cir. Adjust needle size if necessary to obtain the correct gauge.

NOTIONS
Tapestry needle; stitch markers; cable needle (cn); stitch holders.

GAUGE
18 stitches and 27 rows = 4" (10 cm) in stockinette-stitch intarsia color-work pattern from charts on larger needles.

All sizes: Change to larger needle. Beg and ending where indicated for your size, establish patt from Row 1 of charts (pages 42–43) as foll: Work 44 (47, 47) sts of Right Front chart, place marker (pm), work 88 (88, 94) sts of Back chart, pm, work 44 (47, 47) of Left Front chart. Work even in patt from charts until Row 32 (34, 36) has been completed—piece measures about 5¾ (6½, 6¾)" (14.5 [16.5, 17] cm) from CO.

Right Front

Work 44 (47, 47) sts according to Row 33 (35, 37) of Right Front chart, place rem 132 (135, 141) sts on holder for back and left front. On the next WS row, BO 7 sts at beg of row as shown on chart, work in patt to end—37 (40, 40) sts. Cont in patt from chart, BO 1 st at beg of every WS row 8 (9, 10) times, then BO 1 st at beg of every *other* WS row 4 (3, 2) times, ending with Row 66 of chart for all sizes—25 (28, 28) sts rem; piece measures about 10¾ (11¼, 11¼)" (27.5 [28.5, 28.5] cm) from CO. Cont for your size as foll:

Size 39" only: BO 1 st at neck edge (beg of RS rows) on Rows 67, 69, 71, 73, and 75, and *at the same time* BO 1 st at armhole edge (beg of WS rows) on Rows 70 and 74—18 sts rem.

Size 40½" only: BO 1 st at neck edge (beg of RS rows) on Rows 67, 71, 73, and 75, and *at the same time* BO 1 st at armhole edge (beg of WS rows) on Rows 70 and 74—22 sts rem.

Size 41¾" only: BO 1 st at neck edge (beg of RS rows) on Rows 67, 71, and 75, and *at the same time* BO 1 st at armhole edge (beg of WS rows) on Rows 70 and 74—23 sts rem.

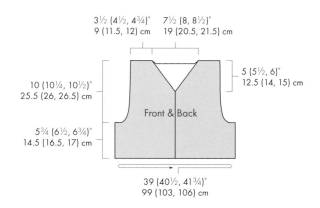

3½ (4½, 4¾)"   7½ (8, 8½)"
9 (11.5, 12) cm   19 (20.5, 21.5) cm

5 (5½, 6)"
12.5 (14, 15) cm

10 (10¼, 10½)"
25.5 (26, 26.5) cm

Front & Back

5¾ (6½, 6¾)"
14.5 (16.5, 17) cm

39 (40½, 41¾)"
99 (103, 106) cm

All sizes: BO 1 st at neck edge every RS row 12 (14, 16) more times, and *at the same time* inc 1 st at armhole edge by working M1 before last st every other RS row 2 (2, 1) time(s), then every RS row 8 (10, 14) times—16 (20, 22) sts rem. Work even in patt until Row 100 (104, 108) has been completed—armhole measures about 10 (10¼, 10½)" (25.5 [26, 26.5] cm) measured straight up along a single column of sts; do not measure along curve of shaped edge. BO all sts.

Back

Return 88 (88, 94) held sts of back to larger needle, and rejoin MC with RS facing. Beg with Row 33 (35, 37) of chart, BO 7 sts at beg of next 2 rows—74 (74, 80) sts rem. Cont in patt from chart, BO 1 st at beg of next 16 (16, 20) rows—58 (58, 60) sts rem. [Work 2 rows even in patt, then BO 1 st at beg of foll 2 rows] 6 (5, 4) times, ending with Row 74 (72, 74) of chart—46 (48, 52) sts rem. Work 2 rows even. Cont for your size as foll:

Sizes 39 (41¾)" only: Inc 1 st at each side on Rows 77 and 81 by working M1 after the first st and before the last st—50 (56) sts.

Size 40½" only: Inc 1 st at each side on Rows 75, 77, and 81 by working M1 after the first st and before the last st—54 sts.

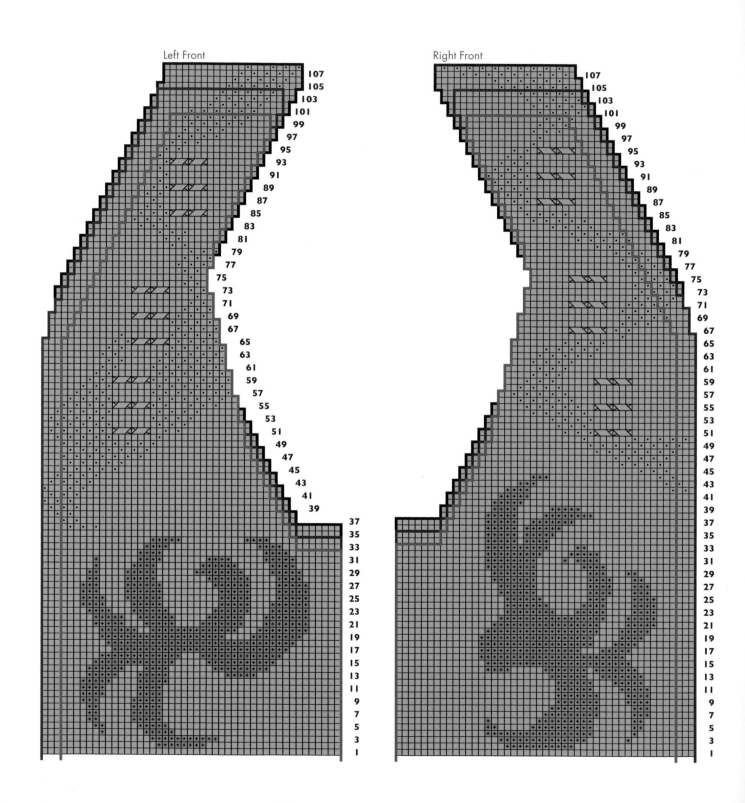

Left Front

107
105
103
101
99
97
95
93
91
89
87
85
83
81
79
77
75
73
71
69
67
65
63
61
59
57
55
53
51
49
47
45
43
41
39
37
35
33
31
29
27
25
23
21
19
17
15
13
11
9
7
5
3
1

Right Front

107
105
103
101
99
97
95
93
91
89
87
85
83
81
79
77
75
73
71
69
67
65
63
61
59
57
55
53
51
49
47
45
43
41
39
37
35
33
31
29
27
25
23
21
19
17
15
13
11
9
7
5
3
1

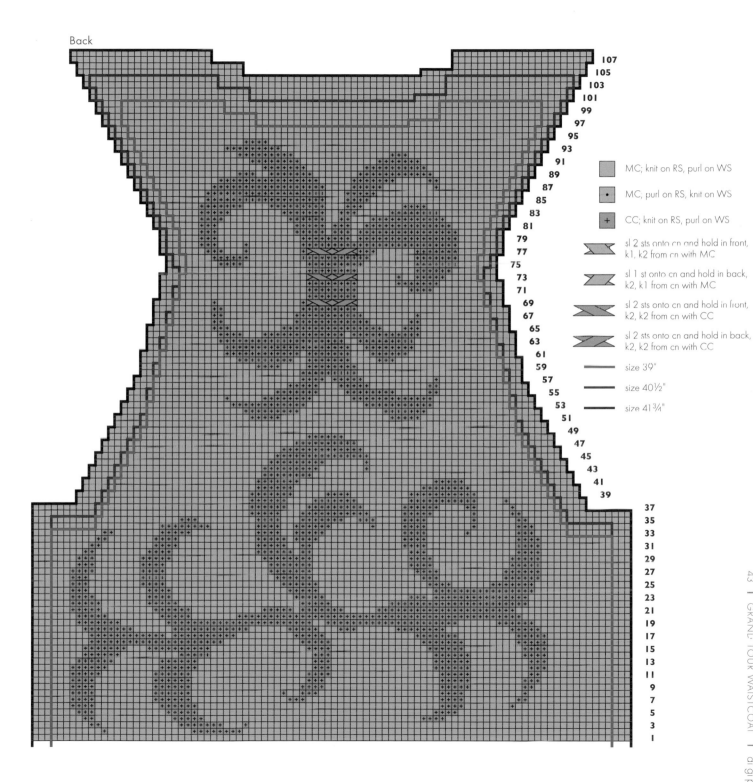

Back

MC; knit on RS, purl on WS

MC, purl on RS, knit on WS

CC; knit on RS, purl on WS

sl 2 sts onto cn and hold in front,
k1, k2 from cn with MC

sl 1 st onto cn and hold in back,
k2, k1 from cn with MC

sl 2 sts onto cn and hold in front,
k2, k2 from cn with CC

sl 2 sts onto cn and hold in back,
k2, k2 from cn with CC

size 39"

size 40½"

size 41¾"

All sizes: Inc 1 st at each side every RS row 7 (9, 11) times, then work 1 WS row even to end with Row 96 (100, 104) of chart)—64 (72, 78) sts.

Mark center 24 (26, 28) sts for back neck. On Row 97 (101, 105) of chart, inc 1 st at beg of row as established, work in patt to marked center sts, join new ball of yarn, BO center 24 (26, 28) sts, work in patt to last st, inc 1 st at end of row—21 (24, 26) sts at each side. Working each side separately, inc 1 st at armhole edge on next 0 (1, 1) RS row(s), and *at the same time* BO 5 sts at each neck edge once—16 (20, 22) sts rem. Work even until Row 100 (104, 108) has been completed—armhole measures about 10 (10¼, 10½)" (25.5 [26, 26.5] cm). BO all sts.

Left Front

Return 44 (47, 47) held sts of left front to larger needle, and rejoin MC with RS facing.

On Row 33 (35, 37) of Left Front chart, BO 7 sts at beg of row, work in patt to end—37 (40, 40) sts rem. Cont in patt from chart, BO 1 st at beg of every RS row 8 (9, 10) times, then BO 1 st at beg of every *other* RS row 4 (3, 2) times, ending with Row 65 of chart for all sizes—25 (28, 28) sts rem; piece measures about 10¾ (11¼, 11¼)" (27.5 [28.5, 28.5] cm) from CO. Cont for your size as foll:

Size 39" only: BO 1 st at neck edge (beg of WS rows) on Rows 66, 68, 70, 72, and 74, and *at the same time* BO 1 st at armhole edge (beg of RS rows) on Rows 69 and 73—18 sts rem.

Size 40½" only: BO 1 st at neck edge (beg of WS rows) on Rows 66, 70, 72, and 74, and *at the same time* BO 1 st at armhole edge (beg of RS rows) on Rows 69 and 73—22 sts rem.

Size 41¾" only: BO 1 st at neck edge (beg of WS rows) on Rows 66, 70, and 74, and *at the same time* BO 1 st at armhole edge (beg of RS rows) on Rows 69 and 73—23 sts rem.

All sizes: BO 1 st at neck edge every WS row 12 (14, 16) more times, and *at the same time* inc 1 st at armhole edge by working M1 after first st every other RS row 2 (2, 1) time(s), then every RS row 8 (10, 14) times—16 (20, 22) sts. Work even in patt until Row 100 (104, 108) has been completed—armhole measures about 10 (10¼, 10½)" (25.5 [26, 26.5] cm) measured straight up along a single column of sts; do not measure along curve of shaped edge. BO all sts.

FINISHING

With MC threaded on a tapestry needle, sew shoulder seams.

Neckband

Join MC to lower right front corner. With longer smaller-size cir needle and RS facing, pick up and knit 68 (72, 74) sts evenly spaced along right front neck to shoulder seam, 37 (39, 41) sts across back neck, and 68 (72, 74) sts along left front from shoulder seam to lower corner of left front—173 (183, 189) sts total. *Next row:* (WS) *K2tog, yo; rep from * to last st, k1. Knit 1 RS row. BO all sts purlwise.

Intarsia allows you to work larger areas without distorting the gauge or producing unnecessarily thick fabric.

Armhole Edging

Join MC to center of BO sts at base of armhole. With shorter smaller-size cir needle and RS facing, pick up and knit 95 (97, 99) sts evenly spaced around armhole. Do not join. *Next row:* (WS) *K2tog, yo; rep from * to last st, k1. Knit 1 RS row. BO all sts purlwise. With MC threaded on a tapestry needle, sew short selvedges of armhole edging tog.

Weave in loose ends. Block to measurements.

Ann Budd was inspired by the Burma Rings Sweater by the late Barbara Venishnick on the cover of the Winter 2000/2001 issue of *Interweave Knits*. She used the concept of stacked rings to create a scarf that would literally wrap around the neck. The plush chenille yarn in rich shades of reds and purples give a sense of royalty—and feels much more luxurious around the neck than a stack of metal rings.

SCARF

With A, CO 310 sts. Beg with a RS row, work back and forth in rows as foll:

Rows 1–5: With A, work 5 rows even in St st (knit RS rows; purl WS rows).

Rows 6–9: With B, work 4 rows even in rev St st (purl RS rows; knit WS rows).

Row 10: (WS; tuck row) Fold last 4 rows in half along purl side of fabric, forming a tuck protruding to the RS to bring Row 5 (last row worked with A) up close to the needle. With B, *insert needle through purl bump of Row 5 directly below next st on needle, then through st on needle, then knit through both loops tog; rep from * to end of row—first tuck completed.

Rows 11–15: With C, rep Rows 1–5.

Rows 16–19: With D, rep Rows 6–9.

Row 20: (WS, tuck row) Fold last 4 rows in half as for Row 10 to bring last row of previous color stripe up close to the needle; when working Row 20 this will be Row 15, the last row worked with C. With D, *insert needle through purl bump of last row of previous color stripe directly below next st on needle, then through st on needle, then knit through both loops; rep from * to end of row.

Rows 21–25: With E, rep Rows 11–15.

Rows 26–30: With A, rep Rows 16–20, using A for tuck Row 30.

Rows 31–35: With B, rep Rows 11–15.

Rows 36–40: With C, rep Rows 16–20, using C for tuck Row 40.

Rows 41–45: With D, rep Rows 11–15.

Rows 46–50: With E, rep Rows 16–20, using E for tuck Row 50.

With A, work 2 rows even in St st. BO all sts.

FINISHING

Weave in loose ends, hiding ends in center of tucks when possible. No blocking is necessary.

FINISHED SIZE
About 3½" (9 cm) wide and 82½" (209.5 cm) long.

YARN
Chunky (#5 Bulky).

Shown here: Crystal Palace Cotton Chenille (100% cotton; 98 yd [89 m]/50 g): #4212 blue-purple (A), 2 skeins; #9719 red-purple (B), #4021 dark red (C), #8166 bright red (D), and #4519 mauve (E), 1 skein each.

NEEDLES
Size 5 (3.75 mm): 40" (100 cm) circular (cir).

NOTIONS
Tapestry needle.

GAUGE
About 15 stitches and 24 rows = 4" (10 cm) in stockinette stitch. Exact gauge is not critical for this project, but differences in gauge may produce a scarf with different finished dimensions.

BUNAD MUKLUKS
ROBIN MELANSON

These woolly mukluks are a fusion of Inuit-style footwear and the embellishments of Norwegian folk costumes. **Robin Melanson** added embroidery, fringe, and multicolored tassels that are typically used to decorate mittens and gloves. "One of the things I find interesting about folk pieces is the elaborate decoration of very simple items, often showing the personality of the creator. In an era where we have such easy access to mass-produced clothing, it's nice to contemplate how, in the past, people spent so much time creating and decorating their clothing, and also to try and re-create the joy of detail that we may have somewhat lost."

NEEDLES
Size 8 (5 mm): set of 5 double-pointed (dpn) and optional 12" (30.5 cm) circular (cir); mukluks can be worked entirely on dpn if preferred. Size 15 (10 mm) or larger: 14" (35.5 cm) straight knitting needle.

NOTIONS
Markers (m); stitch holder; tapestry needle; sharp-point sewing needle; sewing thread; pins; cardboard for making tassels; sharp point embroidery needle; 1 pair suede slipper soles to match foot length (available from www.fibertrends.com; soles shown here were dyed black with fabric dye).

GAUGE
18 stitches and 24 rows = 4" (10 cm) with MC worked in stockinette stitch in the round, before felting; 18 stitches and 28 rows = 4" (10 cm) with MC worked in stockinette stitch in the round, after felting.

CHILDREN'S SIZES

With MC and dpn or cir needle, CO 54 (54, 58, 58, 58) sts. Place marker (pm), and join for working in the rnd, being careful not to twist sts; rnd begins at back of leg.

Leg
[Purl 1 rnd, knit 1 rnd] 6 times, purl 1 rnd, then knit 2 rnds—piece measures about 1¾" (4.5 cm) from CO. *Eyelet rnd:* K3 (3, 2, 2, 2), *yo, k2tog, k4; rep from * to last 3 (3, 2, 2, 2) sts, yo, k2tog, k1 (1, 0, 0, 0). Knit 8 rnds even. *Dec rnd:* Ssk, knit to last 2 sts, k2tog—2 sts dec'd. Knit 11 rnds even. Rep the last 12 rnds 2 more times, then rep dec rnd once more—46 (46, 50, 50, 50) sts rem. Knit 1 rnd, ending 12 sts before end of rnd. Removing end-of-rnd m as you come to it, slip last 12 sts before m and first 12 sts after m onto a single dpn for heel; leave rem 22 (22, 26, 26, 26) sts on cir needle or dpn to work later for instep.

FINISHED SIZE
Children's sizes: 7½ (7¾, 8, 8¼, 8½)" (19 [19.5, 20.5, 21, 21.5] cm) foot length; to fit children's U.S. shoe sizes 11 (12, 12½, 13, 1).
Adult sizes: 9 (9¼, 9½, 9¾, 10, 10¼)" (23 [23.5, 24, 25, 25.5, 26] cm) foot length; to fit women's U.S. shoe sizes 5 (6, 7, 8, 9, 10). Children's mukluks shown measure 8½" (21.5 cm) foot length; adult mukluks shown measure 10" (25.5 cm) foot length.

YARN
Worsted and sportweight (#4 Medium and #2 Fine).

Shown here: Brown Sheep Lamb's Pride Worsted (85% wool, 15% mohair; 190 yd [173 m]/4 oz [113 g]): #M102 orchid thistle (MC, mauve), 2 skeins for children's sizes; #M06 deep charcoal (MC), 3 skeins for adult sizes.

Brown Sheep NatureSpun Sport (100% wool; 184 yd [168 m]/50 g): #205 regal purple (CC1), #880 charcoal (CC2), #110 blueberry (CC3), and #N65 sapphire (CC4), 1 ball each for children's sizes; #110 blueberry (CC1), #207 alpine violet (CC2), #N65 sapphire (CC3), and #205 regal purple (CC4), 1 ball each for adult sizes.

Heel Flap

Work 24 heel flap sts back and forth in rows in garter st (knit every row) for 18 rows, ending with a WS row—heel flap measures about 1½" (3.8 cm).

Turn Heel

Work short-rows (see Glossary, page 156) as foll:

Row 1: (RS) With RS facing, k16 to last 8 sts, ssk, wrap next st, turn.

Row 2: (WS) Knit to last 8 sts, k2tog, wrap next st, turn—wrapped sts are the 6th st in from each end.

Row 3: (RS) Knit to 1 st before previous wrapped st, ssk (wrapped st tog with st before it), wrap next st, turn.

Row 4: (WS) Knit to 1 st before previous wrapped st, k2tog (wrapped st tog with st before it), wrap next st, turn.

Rows 5–12: Rep Rows 3 and 4 four more times—last wrapped st at each side is the edge st.

Row 13: (RS) Knit to last 2 sts, ssk (last wrapped st tog with st before it), turn.

Row 14: (WS) Knit to last 2 sts, k2tog (last wrapped st tog with st before it—10 sts rem.

Shape Gussets

With dpn or cir needle, pick up and knit sts along selvedge edges of heel flap and rejoin for working in the rnd as foll:

Rnd 1: With RS facing, knit the first 5 heel sts, pm to indicate new beg of rnd in center of heel, k5 rem heel sts, pick up and knit 9 sts along selvedge edge of heel flap, k22 (22, 26, 26, 26) instep sts, pick up and knit 9 sts along other selvedge edge of heel flap, knit the first 5 heel sts again—50 (50, 54, 54, 54) sts total. If working on dpn, arrange sts so there are 15 sts each on Needles 1 and 3, and 20 (20, 24, 24, 24) instep sts on Needle 2. If working on a cir needle, pm on each side of center 20 (20, 24, 24, 24) instep sts.

Rnd 2: Knit to last 2 sts of Needle 1 or to 2 sts before first instep m, k2tog, k20 (20, 24, 24, 24) for instep, ssk (first 2 sts of Needle 3 if working on dpn), knit to end—2 sts dec'd.

Rnd 3: Work even.

Rep the last 2 rnds 5 more times—38 (38, 42, 42, 42) sts rem. If working on a cir needle, remove m at each end of instep sts, leaving end-of-rnd m in place.

Foot

Work 23 (25, 27, 29, 31) rnds even in St st—piece measures about 4 (4¼, 4¾, 5, 5¼)" (10 [11, 12, 12.5, 13.5] cm) from last gusset dec rnd.

Don't dismiss an idea before you've tried it.

Begin Toe

Rnd 1: K6 (6, 7, 7, 7), k2tog, pm, k3, pm, ssk, k12 (12, 14, 14, 14), k2tog, pm, k3, pm, ssk, k6 (6, 7, 7, 7)—34 (34, 38, 38, 38) sts rem.

Rnds 2 and 3: Knit 2 rnds even.

Rnd 4: K5 (5, 6, 6, 6), k2tog, k3, ssk, k10 (10, 12, 12, 12), k2tog, k3, ssk, k5 (5, 6, 6, 6)—30 (30, 34, 34, 34) sts.

Rnd 5: Knit 1 rnd even.

Rnd 6: K4 (4, 5, 5, 5), k2tog, k3, ssk, k8 (8, 10, 10, 10), k2tog, k3, ssk, k4 (4, 5, 5, 5)—26 (26, 30, 30, 30) sts.

Rnd 7: K3 (3, 4, 4, 4), k2tog, k3, ssk, k6 (6, 8, 8, 8), k2tog, k3, ssk, do not knit the last 3 (3, 4, 4, 4) sts—22 (22, 26, 26, 26) sts rem.

Redistribute sts on dpn as foll: place unworked 3 (3, 4, 4, 4) sts from end of previous rnd and first 3 (3, 4, 4, 4) sts of foll rnd on 1 dpn for bottom of foot, place 5 sts on each side of foot on a separate dpn, place 6 (6, 8, 8, 8) rem sts on holder to work later for top of foot. Working yarn should be at beg of needle holding sts for bottom of foot.

Finish Toe

Toe is finished by working back and forth in rows across 6 (6, 8, 8, 8) bottom-of-foot sts, and *at the same time* joining them tog with sts from sides of foot as foll:

Row 1: (RS) Knit to last st on bottom-of-foot needle, ssk last st of bottom-of-foot st tog with 1 st from side-of-foot needle—1 st dec'd from side-of-foot needle.

Row 2: (WS) Purl to last st on bottom-of-foot needle, p2tog last bottom-of-foot st tog with 1 st from side-of-foot needle—1 st dec'd from side-of-foot needle.

Rep Rows 1 and 2 four more times until all side sts have been worked—6 (6, 8, 8, 8) sts rem on bottom-of-foot needle. Return 6 (6, 8, 8, 8) held sts for top of foot to dpn. With yarn threaded on a tapestry needle, use the Kitchener st (see Glossary, page 155) to graft sts from bottom-of-foot needle tog with sts from top-of-foot needle.

ADULT SIZES

With MC and dpn or cir needle, CO 70 sts. Place marker (m), and join for working in the rnd, being careful not to twist sts.

Leg

[Purl 1 rnd, knit 1 rnd] 6 times, purl 1 rnd, then knit 2 rnds—piece measures about 1¾" (4.5 cm) from CO. *Eyelet rnd:* K2, *yo, k2tog, k4; rep from * to last 2 sts, yo, k2tog. Knit 4 rnds even. *Dec rnd:* Ssk, knit to last 2 sts, k2tog—2 sts dec'd. Knit 7 rnds even. Rep the last 8 rnds 6 more times, then rep dec rnd once more—54 sts rem. Knit 1 rnd even, ending 14 sts

before end of rnd. Removing end-of-rnd m as you come to it, slip last 14 sts before m and first 14 sts after m onto a single dpn for heel; leave rem 26 sts on dpn or cir needle to work later for instep.

Heel Flap

Work 28 heel flap sts back and forth in rows in garter st (knit every row) for 22 rows, ending with a WS row—heel flap measures about 1¾" (4.5 cm).

Turn Heel

Work short-rows (see Glossary, page 156) as foll:

Row 1: (RS) With RS facing, k19 to last 9 sts, ssk, wrap next st, turn.

Row 2: (WS) Knit to last 9 sts, k2tog, wrap next st, turn—wrapped sts are the 7th st in from each end.

Row 3: (RS) Knit to 1 st before previous wrapped st, ssk (wrapped st tog with st before it), wrap next st, turn.

Row 4: (WS) Knit to 1 st before previous wrapped st, k2tog (wrapped st tog with st before it), wrap next st, turn.

Rows 5–14: Rep Rows 3 and 4 five more times—last wrapped st at each side is the edge st.

Row 15: (RS) Knit to last 2 sts, ssk (last wrapped st tog with st before it), turn.

Row 16: (WS) Knit to last 2 sts, k2tog (last wrapped st tog with st before it), turn—12 sts rem.

Shape Gussets

With dpn or cir needle, pick up and knit sts along selvedge edges of heel flap and rejoin for working in rnds as foll:

Rnd 1: With RS facing, knit the first 6 heel sts, pm to indicate new beg of rnd in center of heel, k6 rem heel sts, pick up and knit 11 sts along selvedge edge of heel flap, k26 instep sts, pick up and knit 11 sts along other selvedge edge of heel flap, knit the first 6 heel sts again—60 sts total. If working on dpn, arrange sts so there are 18 sts each on Needles 1 and 3, and 24 instep sts on Needle 2. If working on a cir needle, pm on each side of center 24 instep sts.

Rnd 2: Knit to last 2 sts of Needle 1 or to 2 sts before first instep m, k2tog, k24 for instep, ssk (first 2 sts on Needle 3 if working on dpn), knit to end—2 sts dec'd.

Rnd 3: Work even.

Rep the last 2 rnds 6 more times—46 sts rem. If working on cir, remove m at each end of instep sts, leaving end-of-rnd m in place.

Foot

Work 29 (31, 33, 35, 37, 39) rnds even in St st—piece measures about 5 (5¼, 5¾, 6, 6¼, 6¾)" (12.5 [13.5, 14.5, 15, 16, 17] cm) from last gusset dec rnd.

BEGIN TOE

Rnd 1: K8, k2tog, pm, k3, pm, ssk, k16, k2tog, pm, k3, pm, ssk, k8—42 sts rem.

Rnds 2 and 3: Knit 2 rnds even.

Rnd 4: K7, k2tog, k3, ssk, k14, k2tog, k3, ssk, k7—38 sts rem.

Rnd 5: Knit 1 rnd even.

Rnd 6: K6, k2tog, k3, ssk, k12, k2tog, k3, ssk, k6—34 sts rem.

Rnd 7: K5, k2tog, k3, ssk, k10, k2tog, k3, ssk, do not knit the last 5 sts—30 sts rem.

Redistribute sts on dpn as foll: place unworked 5 sts from end of previous rnd and first 5 sts of foll rnd on 1 dpn for bottom of foot, place 5 sts on each side of foot on a separate dpn, place rem 10 sts on holder to work later for top of foot. Working yarn should be at beg of needle holding sts for bottom of foot.

Finish Toe

Toe is finished by working back and forth in rows across 10 bottom-of-foot sts, and *at the same time* joining them tog with sts from sides of foot as foll:

Row 1: (RS) Knit to last st on bottom-of-foot needle, ssk last st of bottom-of-foot st tog with 1 st from side-of-foot needle—1 st dec'd from side-of-foot needle.

Row 2: (WS) Purl to last st on bottom-of-foot needle, p2tog last bottom-of-foot st tog with 1 st from side-of-foot needle—1 st dec'd from side-of-foot needle.

Rep Rows 1 and 2 four more times until all side sts have been worked—10 sts rem on bottom-of-foot needle. Return 10 held sts for top of foot to dpn. With yarn threaded on a tapestry needle, use the Kitchener st (see Glossary, page 155) to graft sts from bottom-of-foot needle tog with sts from top-of-foot needle.

FINISHING

Weave in loose ends.

Felting

Felt mukluks according to instructions at left. Shape as desired, placing small towels inside to keep the shape. Poke eyelet holes around top of legs open with large straight knitting needle. Allow to air-dry completely.

Fringe Edging (make 2)

With CC2 and sewing thread held tog, make a slipknot and place on large straight needle. Holding the thread around your thumb and CC2 around your finger, use the long-tail method (see Glossary, page 153) to CO enough sts to pack the straight needle as full as possible, pulling thread very tightly to secure each CO st. When needle is full, cut yarn leaving a 4" (10 cm) tail of yarn and cut thread leaving a 36" (91.5 cm) tail. Using the thread tail on a sewing needle, work whipstitches (see Glossary, page 156) into the CO thread loops all the way across to reinforce base of edging, and fasten off sewing thread. Carefully slip fringe edging from needle. Pin edgings straight to ironing board and press the yarn loops flat with an iron and damp cloth. Pin edgings to inside of top openings of mukluks just below the upper edge, beg and ending at center back leg, and trimming edging so each end extends ¼" to ½" (6 to 13 mm) beyond center back leg. With sewing needle and thread, sew fringe edgings to top of mukluks, folding extensions under so ends meet exactly at center back. Carefully cut open the yarn loops to make fringe, being careful not to cut through the CO sts.

Twisted Cords (make 2)

Cut one strand each of CC2, CC3, and CC4, about 3 yd (2.75 meters) long. With all 3 strands held tog, make twisted cord (see page 150). Thread each cord through eyelets at top of mukluk, beg and ending at center back as shown in photographs.

Tassels

Cut a piece of heavy cardboard to a height of about 3½" (9 cm). For color-block tassels (adult mukluks) using CC2, CC3, and CC4, wind each color 17 times around cardboard, one color after the other. For mixed tassels (children's mukluks) hold all 3 colors tog and wind the 3-strand group 17 times around cardboard. Thread another length of yarn on a tapestry needle, pass needle under all strands at the top edge of the cardboard, and tie the ends of the yarn in a knot on top of the tassel's "head." Wind yarn tightly around the tassel's neck about ½" (1.3 cm) down from top, secure and fasten off. Cut through loops at bottom of tassel and trim ends even. Thread tapestry needle onto one end of twisted cord and pull through top of tassel. Decide how long you would like the twisted cords to be, tie a large knot to hold the tassel on, and trim cord.

Attach Soles

If desired, dye soles (according to dye package directions) to coordinate with yarn colors. Place sole on foot of mukluk and pin in place. With sharp-point sewing needle and matching thread, use a blanket st (see page 148) to sew soles in place. With CC3 threaded on an embroidery needle, sew cross-stitches (see page 148), along the top edge of the soles as shown in photographs.

Embroidery

Using CC3 and sharp-point embroidery needle, work small cross-stitches about 1¼" to 1½" (3.2 to 3.8 cm) apart, centered on garter-stitch upper edge as shown in photographs. Embroider flower motifs for right and left mukluks centered on outside of each leg as shown, about 1" (2.5 cm) below twisted cord on children's sizes, and about 1½" (3.8 cm) below twisted cord on adult sizes. Work closely spaced French knots (see page 149) for flower centers using CC1. Work flower petals in satin stitch (see page 149) using CC2 for inner petals and CC3 for outer petals. Work both halves of leaf in satin stitch using CC4. Work flower stem in stem stitch (see page 149) using CC4.

Embroidery

Left Mukluk   Right Mukluk

ANNIE OAKLEY JACKET
TARA JON MANNING

While helping one of her children research frontier women for a school project, **Tara Jon Manning** became captivated by the life of Annie Oakley—a true American folk hero and an outstanding figure in the history of women's rights. Annie was an accomplished seamstress as well as marksman and was known for her signature shooting outfits. This elegant fitted jacket emulates the style of Annie's hallmark suits and pays tribute to her sewing and embroidery skills.

STITCH GUIDE

Seed Stitch (even number of sts):
Row 1: *K1, p1; rep from * to end of row.
Row 2: Knit the purl sts and purl the knit sts as they appear.
Repeat Row 2 for pattern.

BACK

With MC and smaller straight needles, CO 72 (80, 88, 96, 104) sts. Work in seed st (see Stitch Guide) until piece measures 1½" (3.8 cm) from CO, ending with a WS row. Change to larger straight needles and St st. Cont in St st, and *at the same time* dec 1 st each end of needle every 7th row 6 times—60 (68, 76, 84, 92) sts rem. Cont even in St st until piece measures 8½ (9, 9½, 10, 10½)" (21.5 [23, 24, 25.5, 26.5] cm) from CO, ending with a WS row. Inc 1 st each end of needle on next RS row, then every foll 6th row 4 (4, 3, 3, 3) more times—70 (78, 84, 92, 100) sts. Cont even until piece measures 14 (14½, 16½, 17½, 17½)" (35.5 [37, 42, 44.5, 44.5] cm) from CO, ending with a WS row.

Shape Armholes

BO 4 sts at beg of next 2 rows, then BO 3 sts at beg of foll 2 rows—56 (64, 70, 78, 86) sts rem. Dec 1 st each end of needle every row 2 (3, 4, 6, 8) times—52 (58, 62, 66, 70) sts rem. Cont even until armholes measure 8½ (9, 9½, 9¾, 10)" (21.5 [23, 24, 25, 25.5] cm), ending with a WS row.

Shape Shoulders

BO 7 (8, 8, 9, 9) sts at beg of next 2 rows, then BO 7 (7, 8, 8, 9) sts at beg of foll 2 rows—24 (28, 30, 32, 34) sts rem. BO all sts.

FINISHED SIZE
35 (39, 42, 46, 50)" (89 [99, 106.5, 117, 127] cm) bust circumference, buttoned. Jacket shown measures 39" (99 cm).

YARN
Worsted weight (#4 Medium).
Shown here: Rowan Summer Tweed (70% silk, 30% cotton; 118 yd [108 m]/50 g): #515 raffia (tan, MC), 10 (11, 13, 14, 15) skeins.
Rowan Wool Cotton (50% merino, 50% cotton; 123 yd [112 m]/50 g): #910 gypsy (burgundy), #963 smalt (dark blue), #961 moonstone (light blue), #952 hiss (light purple), and #959 bilberry fool (dark purple), 1 ball each.

NEEDLES
Body and sleeves—size 8 (5 mm): straight. Edging—size 7 (4.5 mm): straight. I-cord—size 5 (3.75 mm): set of 2 double-pointed (dpn). Adjust needle size if necessary to obtain the correct gauge.

NOTIONS
Tapestry needle; pins; tailor's chalk (available from sewing stores); ten ½" (1.3 cm) buttons; sharp-point sewing needle and matching thread for attaching buttons.

GAUGE
16 stitches and 23 rows = 4" (10 cm) in stockinette stitch on largest needles.

LEFT FRONT

With MC and smaller straight needles, CO 36 (40, 44, 48, 52) sts. Work in seed st until piece measures 1½" (3.8 cm) from CO, ending with a WS row. Change to larger straight needles and St st. Cont in St st, and *at the same time* dec 1 st at side edge (beg of RS rows; end of WS rows) every 7th row 6 times—30 (34, 38, 42, 46) sts rem. Cont even in St st until piece measures 8½ (9, 9½, 10, 10½)" (21.5 [23, 24, 25.5, 26.5] cm) from CO, ending with a WS row. Inc 1 st at side edge at beg of next RS row, then every foll 6th row 4 (4, 3, 3, 3) more times—35 (39, 42, 46, 50) sts. Cont even until piece measures 14 (14½, 16½, 17½, 17½)" (35.5 [37, 42, 44.5, 44.5] cm) from CO, ending with a WS row.

Shape Armhole

BO 4 sts at beg of next RS row, then BO 3 sts at beg of foll RS row—28 (32, 35, 39, 43) sts rem. Dec 1 st at armhole edge (beg of RS rows; end of WS rows) every row 2 (3, 4, 6, 8) times—26 (29, 31, 33, 35) sts rem. Cont even until armhole measures 3 (3½, 4, 4¼, 4½)" (7.5 [9, 10, 11, 11.5] cm), ending with a WS row.

Shape Neck

Dec row: (RS) Knit to last 3 sts, k2tog, k1—1 st dec'd at neck edge. Dec 1 st in this manner at end of next 11 (13, 14, 15, 16) RS rows—14 (15, 16, 17, 18) sts rem. Work even in St st if necessary for your size until armhole measures 8½ (9, 9½, 9¾, 10)" (21.5 [23, 24, 25, 25.5] cm), ending with a WS row.

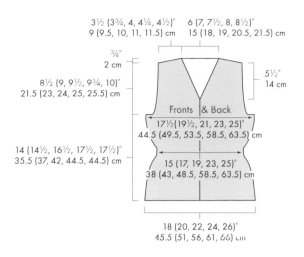

3½ (3¾, 4, 4¼, 4½)"
9 (9.5, 10, 11, 11.5) cm

6 (7, 7½, 8, 8½)"
15 (18, 19, 20.5, 21.5) cm

¾"
2 cm

8½ (9, 9½, 9¾, 10)"
21.5 (23, 24, 25, 25.5) cm

5½"
14 cm

Fronts |& Back

17½(19½, 21, 23, 25)"
44.5 (49.5, 53.5, 58.5, 63.5) cm

14 (14½, 16½, 17½, 17½)"
35.5 (37, 42, 44.5, 44.5) cm

15 (17, 19, 23, 25)"
38 (43, 48.5, 58.5, 63.5) cm

18 (20, 22, 24, 26)"
45.5 (51, 56, 61, 66) cm

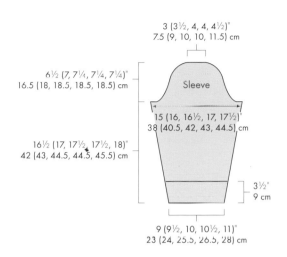

3 (3½, 4, 4, 4½)"
7.5 (9, 10, 10, 11.5) cm

6½ (7, 7¼, 7¼, 7¼)"
16.5 (18, 18.5, 18.5, 18.5) cm

Sleeve

15 (16, 16½, 17, 17½)"
38 (40.5, 42, 43, 44.5) cm

16½ (17, 17½, 17½, 18)"
42 (43, 44.5, 44.5, 45.5) cm

3½"
9 cm

9 (9½, 10, 10½, 11)"
23 (24, 25.5, 26.5, 28) cm

Shape Shoulder

BO 7 (8, 8, 9, 9) sts at beg of next RS row, then BO rem 7 (7, 8, 8, 9) sts at beg of foll RS row.

RIGHT FRONT

With MC and smaller straight needles, CO 36 (40, 44, 48, 52) sts. Work in seed st until piece measures 1½" (3.8 cm) from CO, ending with a WS row. Change to larger straight needles and St st. Cont in St st, and *at the same time* dec 1 st at side edge (end of RS rows, beg of WS rows) every 7th row 6 times—30 (34, 38, 42, 46) sts rem. Cont even in St st until piece measures 8½ (9, 9½, 10, 10½)" (21.5 [23, 24, 25.5, 26.5] cm) from CO, ending with a WS row. Inc 1 st at side edge at end of next RS row, then every foll 6th row 4 (4, 3, 3, 3) more times—35 (39, 42, 46, 50) sts. Cont even until piece measures 14 (14½, 16½, 17½, 17½)" (35.5 [37, 42, 44.5, 44.5] cm) from CO, ending with a RS row.

Shape Armhole

BO 4 sts at beg of next WS row, then BO 3 sts at beg of foll WS row—28 (32, 35, 39, 43) sts rem. Dec 1 st at armhole edge (end of RS rows; beg of WS rows) every row 2 (3, 4, 6, 8) times—26 (29, 31, 33, 35) sts rem. Cont even until armhole measures 3 (3½, 4, 4¼, 4½)" (7.5 [9, 10, 11, 11.5] cm), ending with a WS row.

Shape Neck

Dec row: (RS) K1, ssk, knit to end—1 st dec'd at neck edge. Dec 1 st in this manner at beg of next 11 (13, 14, 15, 16) RS rows—14 (15, 16, 17, 18) sts rem. Work even in St st if necessary for your size until armhole measures 8½ (9, 9½, 9¾, 10)" (21.5 [23, 24, 25, 25.5] cm), ending with a RS row.

Sometimes subtle embellishment is all that's needed to give a folk feel.

Shape Shoulder

BO 7 (8, 8, 9, 9) sts at beg of next WS row, then BO rem 7 (7, 8, 8, 9) sts at beg of foll WS row.

SLEEVES

With MC and smaller straight needles, CO 36 (38, 40, 42, 44) sts. Work in seed st until piece measures 3½" (9 cm) from CO, ending with a WS row. Purl the next RS row for fold line. Change to larger straight needles and St st. Cont in St st, and *at the same time* inc 1 st each end of needle every 6th row 9 (9, 13, 13, 13) times, then every 4th row 3 (4, 0, 0, 0 times)—60 (64, 66, 68, 70) sts. Cont even in St st until piece measures 16½ (17, 17½, 17½, 18)" (42 [43, 44.5, 44.5, 45.5] cm) from fold line, ending with a WS row.

Shape Cap

BO 4 sts at beg of next 2 rows, then BO 3 sts at beg of foll 2 rows—46 (50, 52, 54, 56) sts rem. Dec 1 st at each end of needle every RS row 2 (2, 2, 3, 3) times, then every *other* RS row 6 (6, 7, 6, 6) times—30 (34, 34, 36, 38) sts. Dec 1 st at each end of needle every RS row 0 (1, 0, 1, 1) time(s)—30 (32, 34, 34, 36) sts. BO 2 sts at beg of next 2 rows, then BO 3 sts at beg of foll 2 rows, then BO 4 sts at beg of foll 2 rows—12 (14, 16, 16, 18) sts rem. BO all sts.

FINISHING

Block pieces to measurements. Weave in loose ends. With yarn threaded on a tapestry needle, sew fronts to back at shoulders. Sew sleeve caps into armholes. Sew sleeve and side seams, reversing the seam for each seed-st cuff so seam allowances will not show on RS when cuffs are folded up.

Button Band

With MC and RS facing, using smaller straight needles and beg at start of V-neck shaping on left front, pick up and knit 70 (74, 84, 88, 90) sts evenly spaced along left front edge to lower edge. Work in seed st for 9 rows. Loosely BO all sts.

Buttonhole Band

Mark positions for 10 buttonholes on right front edge, the lowest ½" (1.3 cm) up from CO, the highest ½" (1.3 cm) below start of V-neck shaping, and the rem 8 evenly spaced in between. With MC, RS facing, smaller straight needles, and beg at CO lower edge of right front, pick up and knit 70 (74, 84, 88, 90) sts evenly spaced along right front edge start of V-neck shaping. Work in seed st for 4 rows, ending with a RS row. On the next WS row, work in seed st, working (yo, p2tog) for buttonhole at each marked position. Work even in seed st for 4 more rows. Loosely BO all sts.

Collar

With MC and smaller straight needles, CO 86 (92, 94, 98, 100) sts. Work even in seed st until piece measures 1" (2.5 cm) from CO. Dec 1 st at each end of needle every row 30 times—26 (32, 34, 38, 40) sts rem; piece measures about 5" (12.5 cm) from CO measured straight up along a single column of sts at center. BO all sts. Match center of collar CO edge to center of back neck and pin in place. Easing in any fullness, pin rest of collar CO edge to neck edge, then pin 1" (2.5 cm) selvedges of collar to short selvedges at tops of button and buttonhole bands. With yarn threaded on a tapestry needle and working from center back outward, sew collar in place.

Cuff Trim

With burgundy and dpn, CO 6 sts. Work 6 st I-cord (see Glossary, page 155) until piece fits around CO edge of sleeve cuff. BO all sts. With burgundy threaded on a tapestry needle, sew CO and BO ends of I-cord tog. Sew cord to CO edge of sleeve, matching seams.

Embroidery

With tailor's chalk, trace one half of floral embroidery pattern below onto each lower front as shown in photograph, with the lowest embroidery elements positioned about 3½" (9 cm) up from CO edge. Fold back cuffs to RS of garment along fold line and trace one half of floral embroidery pattern onto the RS of each cuff, with closest embroidery element about 1" (2.5 cm) away from I-cord trim. With light blue threaded on a tapestry needle, embroider stems with chain stitch (see pages 148 and 149 for embroidery stitches). With dark blue, work a line of small running stitches close to the stems to shadow them, working the dark blue lines above the stems on the fronts and below the stems on the cuffs as shown. Work leaves in single lazy daisy stitches using a double strand of light blue. Work flower buds as single lazy daisy stitches using a double strand of light purple, with a French knot in dark purple at the center of each bud. Work large flowers as five lazy daisy stitches clustered together using a double strand of light purple, then outline each flower with backstitches using a double strand of dark purple as shown. Work random French knots close to stems using dark purple as shown. With MC threaded on tapestry needle, tack cuffs in place along sleeve seam. Sew buttons to left front, opposite buttonholes.

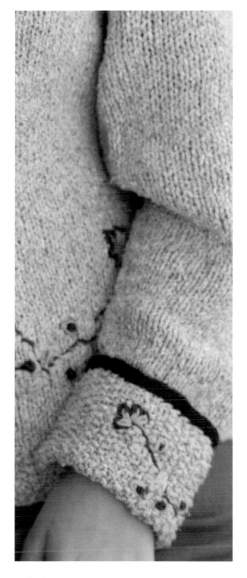

Embroidery

Left Front and
Left Sleeve

Right Front and
Right Sleeve

Gina Wilde's passion for basketmaking prompted the idea for this unusual felted tote. "I rambled all over Tennessee, up into the Smoky Mountains of North Carolina, and even met a few Chickasaw Indians from Mississippi, all in hopes of learning weaving techniques from the few remaining masters of the trade. Basketweaving is a part of the culture of the South that is fast slipping away, and I am grateful for learning to weave at the source." Incorporating motifs of the Southwest's Pima Native American tribe, Gina's Intentions to synthesize two distinctly North American "tribes" of weavers hits the mark with this knitted tribute to American basketry.

NOTES

❖ You may find it helpful to use a marker in a color different from the rest to indicate the beginning of the round and markers in yet another color to set off the individual motifs of Chart 2.

❖ To ensure that loose ends do not work themselves free during felting, trim the ends of each color to 3"–4" (7.5–10 cm) long and weave them in as you go.

❖ Keep your tension even while working two-color pattern sections and twist the yarns around each other every 2–3 stitches to avoid long floats across the back of the work.

BASE

With A and cir needle, CO 18 sts. Do not join. Working back and forth in rows, work 2 rows in garter st (knit every row). Cont as foll:

Row 1: (RS) K1, knit into front and back of next st (k1f&b), knit to last 2 sts, k1f&b, k1—2 sts inc'd.

Row 2: Knit.

Rep Rows 1 and 2 five more times—30 sts. Cont even in garter st until piece measures 5½" (14 cm) from CO, ending with a WS row. Cont as foll:

Row 1: (RS) K1, k2tog, knit to last 2 sts, k2tog, k1—2 sts dec'd.

Row 2: Knit.

Rep these 2 rows 5 more times—18 sts rem.

FINISHED SIZE

After felting, about 8" (20.5 cm) wide at base, 15½" (39.5 cm) wide at top, and 12¼" (31 cm) tall. Before felting, about 9½" (24 cm) wide at base, 16¼" (41.5 cm) wide at top, and 15½" (39.5 cm) tall.

YARN

DK weight (#3 Light).

Shown here: Alchemy Yarns Sanctuary (70% merino, 30% silk; 125 yd [114 m]/50 g): #76E citrine (light olive; A), 2 skeins; #35E fauna (dark olive; B), #96E two rock (brown; C), #36F lantern (gold; D), #72E vintage jade (pale jade; E), and #48A passion flower (purple; F), 1 skein each.

NEEDLES

Size 6 (4 mm): 16" (40 cm) circular (cir) and set of 4 or 5 double-pointed (dpn). Adjust needle size if necessary to obtain the correct gauge.

NOTIONS

Markers (m; 2 or 3 colors recommended); tapestry needle; pillow case or lingerie bag for machine felting; bath towels; straight pins; one pair of 6"–8" (15–20.5 cm) handles (handles shown are from The Knitterly in Petaluma, California); sharp-point sewing needle and matching thread for attaching handles.

GAUGE

Before felting, about 20 stitches and 34 rows = 4" (10 cm) in garter stitch; about 16 stitches and 20 rounds = 3" (7.5 cm) in stockinette stitch worked in the round.

Sides

Pick up sts from around the outer edge of base as foll: With A already attached and RS of base facing, place marker (pm) in color to indicate beg of rnd, knit across 18 sts on needle for base, pm for corner, pick up and knit 8 sts along decreased selvedge, 16 sts along straight selvedge, and 8 sts along increased selvedge, pm for corner, pick up and knit 18 sts across CO edge of base, pm for corner, pick up and knit 8 sts along increased selvedge, 16 sts along straight selvedge, and 8 sts along rem decreased selvedge—100 sts total.

Rnds 1–3: With A, knit 3 rnds.

Rnds 4 and 5: Change to B and knit 1 rnd, then purl 1 rnd.

Rnd 6: (inc rnd) With B, knit to first corner m, sl m, k1f&b, knit to last st before next corner m, k1f&b, sl m, k18, sl m, k1f&b, knit to last st before end-of-rnd m, k1f&b—104 sts.

Rnds 7 and 8: With B, knit 2 rnds.

Rnd 9: Join F, *k3 with B, k1 with F; rep from * to end.

Rnd 10: K1 with F, *k1 with B, k3 with F; rep from * to last 3 sts, k1 with B, k2 with F.

Rnd 11: Rep Rnd 9.

Chart 1

	7
	5
	3
	1

Chart 2

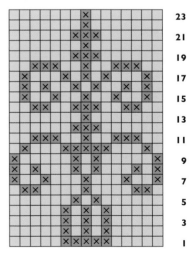

	23
	21
	19
	17
	15
	13
	11
	9
	7
	5
	3
	1

	light olive
■	brown
	pale jade green
×	dark olive
☐	pattern repeat

Rnd 12: (inc rnd) With B, rep Rnd 6—108 sts.

Rnds 13–15: With B, knit 3 rnds.

Rnds 16 and 17: With B, knit 1 rnd, then purl 1 rnd.

Rnd 18: (inc rnd) With D, rep Rnd 6—112 sts.

Rnd 19: With D, purl 1 rnd.

Rnds 20 and 21: With E, knit 1 rnd, then purl 1 rnd.

Rnds 22 and 23: With C, knit 1 rnd, then purl 1 rnd.

Rnd 24: (inc rnd) With A, rep Rnd 6—116 sts.

Rnds 25–28: With A, knit 4 rnds.

Rnd 29: (inc rnd) with A, rep Rnd 6—120 sts.

Rnds 30–36: With A and C, work Rnds 1–7 of Chart 1.

Rnd 37: (inc rnd) With A, rep Rnd 6—124 sts.

Rnds 38–41: With A, knit 4 rnds—piece measures about 6¼" (16 cm) from pick-up rnd.

Rnd 42: (inc rnd) With F, rep Rnd 6—128 sts.

Rnd 43: With F, purl 1 rnd.

Rnds 44 and 45: With B, knit 1 rnd, then purl 1 rnd.

Rnds 46 and 47: With D, knit 1 rnd, then purl 1 rnd.

Rnd 48: (inc rnd) With A, rep Rnd 6—132 sts.

Rnd 49: With A, purl 1 rnd.

Rnds 50–52: With E, knit 3 rnds.

Rnd 53: (inc rnd) With E, rep Rnd 6—136 sts; 2 groups of 18 sts each for sides of bag, and 2 groups of 50 sts each for front and back of bag.

Rnd 54: Establish position of motifs from Chart 2, using different-colored markers if desired to separate the motifs from the background. *Work 18-st group for side of bag as k2 with E, pm, work Rnd 1 of chart over next 15 sts, pm, k1 with E, sl m at end of 18-st group; work 50-st group for front or back of bag as k5 with E, pm, work Rnd 1 of chart over next 15 sts, pm, k10 with E, pm, work Rnd 1 of chart over next 15 sts, pm, k5 with E, sl m at end of 50-st group; rep from * once more—6 marked 15-st chart sections. There will be 1 chart section centered as well as possible on each 18-st side group and 2 chart sections on each 50-st front or back group positioned 5 sts in from each end with 10 sts between chart sections at center.

Rnds 55–76: Work Rnds 2–23 of Chart 2, working background sts outside chart sections with E. *At the same time,* inc 6 sts on Rnds 6, 12, 17, and 23 of chart (Rnds 59, 65, 70, and 76 of bag) by inc 1 st at each corner as established for Rnd 6, and also inc 1 st in middle of both front and back by working k1f&b with E as close as possible to the center of the sts between the 2 chart sections—160 sts after completing Rnd 23 of chart (Rnd 76 of bag); 2 groups of 18 sts each for sides of bag and 2 groups of 62 sts each for front and back of bag. The marked chart sections on front and back will be positioned 9 sts in from each end

with 14 sts between chart sections at center. Remove m for chart sections as you come to them on next rnd. Do not remove the corner m at each end of the front and back because they will still be needed for shaping.

Rnds 77–79: With E, knit 3 rnds.

Rnd 80: (inc rnd) With C, rep Rnd 6—164 sts.

Rnd 81: With C, purl 1 rnd.

Rnds 82 and 83: With F, knit 1 rnd, then purl 1 rnd.

Rnds 84 and 85: With A, knit 1 rnd, then purl 1 rnd.

Rnd 86: (inc rnd) With B, rep Rnd 6—168 sts.

Rnd 87: With B, purl 1 rnd.

Rnds 88–90: With F, knit 3 rnds.

Rnd 91: Join D, and *k3 with F, k1 with D; rep from * to end.

Rnd 92: K1 with D, *k1 with F, k3 with D; rep from * to last 3 sts, k1 with F, k2 with D.

Rnd 93: Rep Rnd 91.

Rnd 94: (inc rnd) With F, rep Rnd 6—172 sts.

Rnds 95 and 96: With F, knit 2 rnds.

Rnds 97 and 98: With B, knit 1 rnd, then purl 1 rnd.

Rnds 99–104: With A, [knit 1 rnd, then purl 1 rnd] 3 times—piece measures about 15½" (39.5 cm) from pick-up rnd. BO all sts with A.

HANDLE FASTENER

With C and dpn, CO 5 sts. Work in garter st until piece measures 40" (101.5 cm) from CO. BO all sts. *Note:* After felting, this piece will be cut into four sections about 7" (18 cm) long each that will be used to attach handles.

FINISHING

Weave in rem loose ends.

Felting

Note: Felt bag and handle fastener piece separately. Exact size is determined by felting time, so be sure to check bag frequently (every 5 minutes) while in the washing machine. The amount of time needed to satisfactorily felt the bag depends on yarn, water temperature, water hardness, and amount of agitation. Place bag in pillowcase or lingerie bag to protect washing machine from loose fibers. Set water for hottest temperature, lowest water level, and most gentle agitation. Add a very small amount of quality laundry detergent. Check progress every 5 minutes and carefully reset the machine cycle back to agitate so it does not accidentally progress to the spin cycle. When the bag appears to be the right size, remove from washer, hand-rinse in cold water, then roll in towels to remove excess water. Shape by hand,

Practice new color-work techniques with felting in mind—distorted stitches and small holes will disappear "in the wash."

pulling any color-work sections that might have contracted during the felting process to the correct width. Allow to air-dry over a similarly shaped object (a tall flower vase was used here). Felt handle fastener piece in the same manner.

Assembly

Cut handle fastener into four equal pieces. Identify the center of the front and back sides. Using the distance between the handle loops as a guide, mark location for four handle fasteners, two each on front and back. Slip each handle fastener through a handle ring, fold fastener in half, and pin in place close to handle loop. Place each fastener at a marked handle position, sandwich the upper bag between the halves of the fastener, and pin in place. With sharp-point sewing needle and thread, sew fasteners to bag on inside and outside, stitching through all layers.

A Moroccan flat-top fez served as the springboard for **Kristin Nicholas's** joyful topper. She worked the body of the hat in two-color stranded knitting. Kristin turned to her passion for simple, naïve stitchery to add bright accent colors. To mix the folk with the familiar, she intertwined sunflower motifs inspired by the traditional floral patterns of Suzani textiles from Uzbekistan and ones fresh from her own garden.

FINISHED SIZE
21½" (54 cm) circumference. To fit an adult.

YARN
Worsted weight (#4 Medium).
Shown here: Nashua Handknits Julia (50% wool, 25% alpaca, 25% mohair; 93 yd [85 m]/50 g): #1220 tarnished brass (gold, A), #8141 pretty pink (B), #6396 deep blue sea (dark teal, C), and #3961 ladies mantle (green, D), 1 ball each.

NEEDLES
Sizes 5 (3.75 mm) and 7 (4.5 mm): set of four or five double-pointed; a 16" (40 cm) circular (cir) needle may be used for the brim. Adjust needle size if necessary to obtain the correct gauge.

NOTIONS
Marker (m); tapestry needle.

GAUGE
17 stitches and 24 rows = 4" (10 cm) in stockinette stitch using larger needles.

> **NOTE**
> ❖ Take care to strand yarn loosely across the back of the work when knitting the flower centers to maintain a consistent gauge. If you find that your two-color knitting usually puckers, try using even larger needles when doing stranded color-work.

HAT

Brim

With A and smaller needles, CO 80 sts. Place marker (pm) and join for working in the rnd, being careful not to twist sts.

Rnds 1 and 2: Purl.

Work 2-color garter st on Rnds 3 and 4 as foll:

Rnd 3: *K2 with B, k2 with C; rep from * to end.

Rnd 4: *Bring B to front, p2 with B, bring B to back, bring C to front, p2 with C, bring C to back; rep from * to end.

Rnds 5–7: With D, knit 1 rnd, then purl 2 rnds.

Rnd 8: With C, knit 1 rnd, inc 10 sts evenly spaced—90 sts.

Rnds 9–15: With C, knit 7 rnds.

Work flower centers in 2-color stranded St st on Rnds 16–20 (see Note) as foll:

Rnd 16: K6 with C, *k3 with B, k7 with C; rep from * to last 4 sts, k3 with B, k1 with C.

Rnds 17–19: *K5 with C, k5 with B; rep from *.

Rnd 20: Rep Rnd 16.

Rnds 21–30: With C, knit 10 rnds.

Rnd 31: With A, knit 1 rnd, inc 1 st—91 sts.

Rnds 32–34: With A, purl 3 rnds—piece measures about 5¼" (13.5 cm) from CO.

Brighten up a cold-
weather garment
with bright whimsical
accents.

Crown

Dec for crown as foll:

Rnd 35: With C, *k2tog, k11; rep from *—84 sts rem.

Rnd 36: With C, knit 1 rnd.

Rnd 37: With B, *k2tog, k10; rep from *—77 sts rem.

Rnds 38–40: With B, purl 3 rnds.

Rnd 41: With C, *k2tog, k9; rep from *—70 sts rem.

Rnd 42: With C, knit 1 rnd.

Rnd 43: With D, *k2tog, k8; rep from *—63 sts rem.

Rnds 44–46: Purl 3 rnds.

Change to C, and work Rnds 47–56 with C.

Rnd 47: *K2tog, k7; rep from *—56 sts rem.

Rnds 48, 50, 52, and 54: Knit.

Rnd 49: *K2tog, k6; rep from *—49 sts rem.

Rnd 51: *K2tog, k5; rep from *—42 sts rem.

Rnd 53: *K2tog, k4; rep from *—35 sts rem.

Rnd 55: *K2tog, k3; rep from *—28 sts rem.

Rnd 56: With C, knit 1 rnd.

Change to B, and work to end with B.

Rnd 57: *K2tog, k2; rep from *—21 sts rem.

Rnds 58 and 60: Knit 1 rnd.

Rnd 59: *K2tog, k1; rep from *—14 sts rem.

Rnd 61: *K2tog; rep from *—7 sts rem. Break yarn and use tapestry needle to thread tail through rem sts. Pull tight to close hole at top of hat, and secure tail on WS.

FINISHING

Weave in loose ends.

Turn hat inside out. Identify the rev St st stripe in A formed by Rnds 31–32, just below the start of the crown shaping. When viewed from the WS, there will be lines of purl "dots" above and below the stripe where the colors changed. Fold the stripe in half so these lines of dots are touching, and with A threaded on a tapestry needle, whipstitch (see Glossary, page 156) the dotted purl lines tog to form a raised rev St st ridge on the RS of the hat.

Embroidery

Using A and D randomly, work 12 daisy stitches (see page 149) around each flower center as shown, working shorter sts between the flower centers and larger sts above and below the flower centers. With A, work 13 daisy sts radiating out from the B section at top of crown, each about 1¼" (3.2 cm) long, to form a flower motif on the top of the hat.

SHANGHAI SURPLICE
ANNIE MODESITT

Annie Modesitt was inspired by the shape of a fifteenth-century quilted vest from China. True to Folk Style form, this knitted vest marries duplicate stitch and European French-knot embroidery techniques with Asian shaping. The faux surplice silhouette is created with short-row shaping; a crochet button creates more illusion at the base of the Mandarin collar. An unusual I-cord technique creates the strong diagonal and horizontal lines of this detailed garment.

STITCH GUIDE

Horizontal I-Cord: *Using the cable method (see Glossary, page 152), CO 1 st but do not transfer the new st to the left needle, knit the next 2 sts on left needle, ssk, return the last 3 sts worked to left needle, leaving the new CO st on right needle, bring yarn around the back of the I-cord in position to work a RS row again; rep from * until all sts have been worked—stitch count should be the same as when you started; the CO st at beg of each rep replaces the st dec'd by the ssk join. *Note:* Depending on how loosely you work the CO, the new sts may appear slightly more elongated than regular St st, producing a deliberate decorative effect.

I-Cord Bind-Off: With RS tacing and using the cable method, CO 2 sts at beg of row. *K2, ssk; return 3 sts just worked to left needle, bring yarn around the back of the I-cord in position to work a RS row again; rep from * until 3 sts rem, sssk (see Glossary, page 154)—1 st rem. Fasten off last st.

BODY

With light brown and longer needle, use the provisional method (see Glossary, page 153) to CO 175 (200, 225, 250, 275, 300) sts. Do *not* join. Working back and forth in rows, knit 2 rows with light brown. *Next row:* (RS) Set up patt from Row 1 of Scrollwork chart (page 76; see Notes) as foll: Beg where indicated for your size, work last 13 (0, 13, 0, 13, 0) sts of chart once, rep entire 50-st patt 3 (4, 4, 5, 5, 6) times, then work first 12 (0, 12, 0, 12, 0) sts of chart once. Work Rows 2–16 of Scrollwork chart as established. With light brown, knit 4 rows. *Next row:* (RS) With olive, work horizontal I-cord (see Stitch Guide). Knit 1 WS row with olive, knit 2 rows with light brown, then knit 2 rows with plum, ending with a WS row—piece measures about 4¼" (11 cm) from CO. *Next row:* (RS) Set up patt from Row 1 of Flower chart (see Notes) as foll: Place first 25 sts of row on holder for left front for all sizes, join light brown

FINISHED SIZE
30½ (35, 39, 44, 48, 52½)" (77.5 [89, 99, 112, 122, 133.5] cm) bust circumference. Vest shown measures 35" (89 cm).

YARN
Sportweight (#2 Fine).

Shown here: Brown Sheep Cotton Fine (80% cotton, 20% wool; 222 yd [203 m]/50 g). #CW820 teddy bear (light brown, A), 6 (6, 8, 9, 10, 10) balls; #CW 475 olivette (olive, B), 4 (4, 4, 4, 5, 5) balls; #CW832 silver plum (C), 3 (3, 4, 4, 4, 4) balls, #CW455 willow leaf (yellow-green, D), 2 (2, 2, 2, 3, 3) balls.

NEEDLES
Size 7 (4.5 mm): 16" and 24" (40 and 60 cm) circular (cir). Adjust needle size if necessary to obtain the correct gauge.

NOTIONS
Marker (m); stitch holders; tapestry needle; size F/5 (3.75 mm) crochet hook; one ⅝" (1.5 cm) button.

GAUGE
21 stitches and 30 rows = 4" (10 cm) in stockinette-stitch intarsia patterns from charts.

❖ The lower body is worked back and forth in rows in one piece to the waist, then stitches are put on hold for the left front, and the right front and back are worked in one piece to the right armhole. After dividing for the armhole, the right front and back are worked separately to the shoulders. The roughly C-shaped left front insert is worked by picking up stitches along the curved edge of the right front and working out toward the left side, armhole, and shoulder.

❖ The purl stitches of the Scrollwork chart provide a guide for working the chain stitch and French knot embroidery on the lower band and left front. The embroidery is shown on page 78.

❖ The olive and yellow-green stems of the Flower chart may be worked in stockinette-stitch intarsia, using a separate length of yarn for each color section and crossing yarns at each color change to avoid leaving holes. As an alternative, you can work the chart entirely in stockinette using the background color and embroider the stems later in duplicate stitch, using the chart as a guide. The positions of the French knot flower buds are shown on the chart for reference; work these stitches in stockinette using the background color and embroider the French knots where indicated after the knitting is finished.

and other colors as needed, work 25-st rep of chart 6 (7, 8, 9, 10, 11) times, and *at the same time* place a marker (pm) when there are 62 (75, 88, 100, 113, 125) sts on right needle to indicate right side and beg of back—150 (175, 200, 225, 250, 275) sts rem; with RS facing, 62 (75, 87, 100, 112, 125) sts before m for right front, and 88 (100, 113, 125, 138, 150) sts after m for back. *Next row:* (WS) Work in established patt from Row 2 of chart to last 3 sts, p2tog, p1—1 st dec'd at right front neck edge. *Next row:* (RS) K1, k2tog, work in established patt from Row 3 of chart to end—1 st dec'd at right front neck edge. Work Rows 4–18 of chart as established, and *at the same time* dec 1 st at right front neck edge (end of WS rows; beg of RS rows) every row, working decs at end of each rep on Rows 5 and 9 as shown on chart—121 (144, 167, 190, 213, 236) sts rem when Row 18 has been completed; 17 sts total removed from neck edge; 25-st rep has been decreased to 23-st rep; with RS facing, 41 (52, 64, 75, 87, 98) sts before m for right front, and 80 (92, 103, 115, 126, 138) sts after m for back. *Note:* From this point on, rep only Rows 19–62 of Flower chart for patt to end of back and right front; do not work Rows 1–18 again. Cont in patt, and *at the same time* dec 1 st at right front neck edge every row 2 (7, 13, 17, 21, 21) more times—119 (137, 154, 173, 192, 215) sts; 39 (45, 51, 58, 66, 77) front sts, still 80 (92, 103, 115, 126, 138) back sts. Cont even in patt until piece measures 8 (8, 8½, 9, 9½, 9½)" (20.5 [20.5, 21.5, 23, 24, 24] cm) from CO, ending with a WS row. *Note:* Lower border will add an additional ¾" (2 cm) in length when it is applied during finishing.

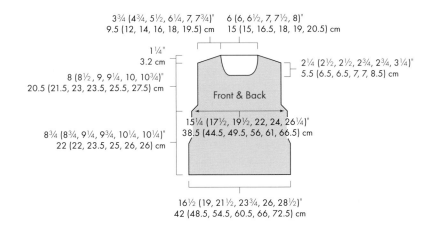

3¾ (4¾, 5½, 6¼, 7, 7¾)"
9.5 (12, 14, 16, 18, 19.5) cm

6 (6, 6½, 7, 7½, 8)"
15 (15, 16.5, 18, 19, 20.5) cm

1¼"
3.2 cm

2¼ (2½, 2½, 2¾, 2¾, 3¼)"
5.5 (6.5, 6.5, 7, 7, 8.5) cm

8 (8½, 9, 9¼, 10, 10¾)"
20.5 (21.5, 23, 23.5, 25.5, 27.5) cm

Front & Back

15¼ (17½, 19½, 22, 24, 26¼)"
38.5 (44.5, 49.5, 56, 61, 66.5) cm

8¾ (8¾, 9¼, 9¾, 10¼, 10¼)"
22 (22, 23.5, 25, 26, 26) cm

16½ (19, 21½, 23¾, 26, 28½)"
42 (48.5, 54.5, 60.5, 66, 72.5) cm

BACK

Dividing row: (RS) Work in patt to side m, place 39 (45, 51, 58, 66, 77) sts just worked on holder for right front, remove side m, work first 5 back sts with light brown as k3, ssk, work in established patt from chart to last 5 sts, with light brown k2tog, k3 —2 sts dec'd. *Next row:* (WS) Work first 5 sts with light brown as p3, p2tog, work in established patt from chart to last 5 sts, with light brown ssp (see Glossary, page 154), p3—2 sts dec'd. Cont in patt from chart, dec 1 st at each side in the same manner on the next 2 (3, 3, 4, 4, 5) rows—72 (82, 93, 103, 114, 124) sts rem. Cont even in patt until armholes measure 8 (8½, 9, 9¼, 10, 10¾)" (20.5 [21.5, 23, 23.5, 25.5, 27.5] cm) from dividing row, ending with a WS row.

Shape Shoulders

Work short-rows (see Glossary, page 156) as foll:

Rows 1 and 2: Work in patt to last 4 (6, 8, 8, 9, 10) sts, wrap next st, turn

Rows 3–6: Work in patt to 5 (6, 7, 8, 9, 10) sts before previous wrapped st, wrap next st, turn.

Rows 7 and 8: Work in patt to 6 (7, 7, 9, 10, 11) sts before previous wrapped st, wrap next st, turn—last wrapped st at each side is the 20 (25, 29, 33, 37, 41)th st in from each edge. Working wrapped sts tog with their wraps as you come to them, BO 20 (25, 29, 33, 37, 41) sts at beg of next 2 rows—32 (32, 35, 37, 40, 42) sts rem for back neck. Place sts on holder.

RIGHT FRONT

Return 39 (45, 51, 58, 66, 77) right front sts to longer cir needle and rejoin yarns with WS facing. *Next row:* (WS) Work first 5 sts with light brown as p3, p2tog, work in established patt from chart to end—1 st dec'd. *Next row:* (RS) Work in established patt to last 5 sts, with light brown k2tog, k3 —1 st dec'd. Cont in patt from chart, dec 1 st at armhole edge (beg of WS rows; end of RS rows) in the same manner on the next 2 (3, 3, 4, 6, 12) rows—35 (40, 46, 52, 58, 63) sts rem. Cont even in patt until armhole measures 5¾ (6, 6½, 6½, 7¼, 7½)" (14.5 [15, 16.5, 16.5, 18.5, 19] cm), ending with a WS row.

Shape Neck

At neck edge (beg of RS rows), BO 3 (3, 5, 5, 5, 6) sts once, then BO 2 sts 3 (3, 3, 4, 5, 5) times, then dec 1 st at neck edge every row 6 times —20 (25, 29, 33, 37, 41) sts rem. Cont even in patt until armhole measures 8 (8½, 9, 9¼, 10, 10¾)" (20.5 [21.5, 23, 23.5, 25.5, 27.5] cm) from dividing row, ending with a WS row.

Shape Shoulder

Work short-rows as foll:

Row 1: (RS) Work in patt to last 4 (6, 8, 8, 9, 10) sts, wrap next st, turn.

Rows 2, 4, and 6: (WS) Work in patt to end.

Rows 3 and 5: Work in patt to 5 (6, 7, 8, 9, 10) sts before previous wrapped st, wrap next st, turn.

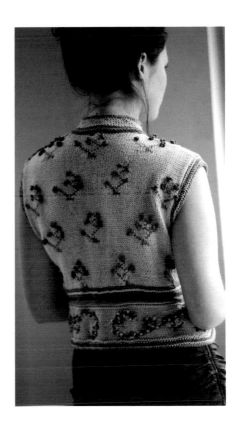

Can't find the right button? Make your own!

Scrollwork

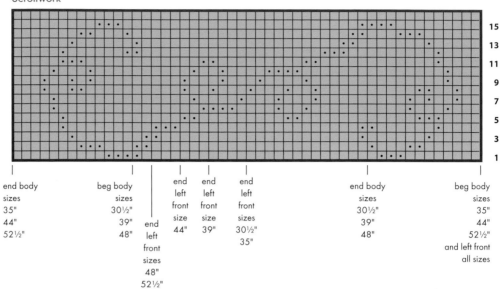

end body sizes 35" 44" 52½"	beg body sizes 30½" 39" 48"	end left front sizes 48" 52½"

end left front size 44"

end left front size 39"

end left front sizes 30½" 35"

end body sizes 30½" 39" 48"

beg body sizes 35" 44" 52½" and left front all sizes

▦	light brown; k on RS, p on WS
▪	light brown; p on RS, k on WS
╱	k2tog with light brown
╲	ssk with light brown
☐	pattern repeat
⊠	olive; k on RS, p on WS, or work later in duplicate st
⊙	yellow-green; k on RS, p on WS, or work later in duplicate st
⬤	light brown; k on RS, p on WS, then embroider French knot with plum

Flower

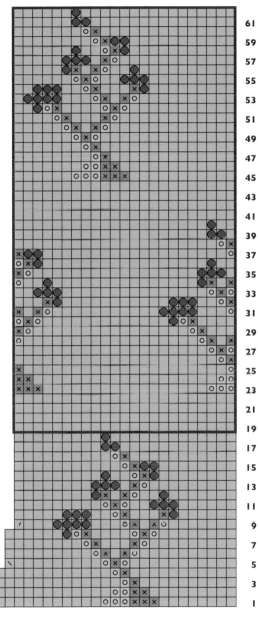

Row numbers (right side of chart, top to bottom): 61, 59, 57, 55, 53, 51, 49, 47, 45, 43, 41, 39, 37, 35, 33, 31, 29, 27, 25, 23, 21, 19, 17, 15, 13, 11, 9, 7, 5, 3, 1

Rows 7 and 8: Work in patt across all sts, working wrapped sts tog with their wraps as you come to them on Row 7.

BO all sts.

LEFT FRONT

Return 25 held sts of lower left front to longer cir needle and join plum with RS facing. *Next row:* (RS) K25, pick up and knit 50 (50, 54, 57, 60, 60) sts evenly spaced along curved right front edge to beg of neck shaping—75 (75, 79, 82, 85, 85) sts total. Knit 1 WS row. Change to light brown and knit 2 rows. Change to olive and work horizontal I-cord. With olive, knit 1 WS row, then knit 4 rows with light brown, ending with a WS row.

Shape Neck

Next row: (RS) Set up patt from Row 1 of Scrollwork chart as foll: Work entire 50-st patt once, then work first 25 (25, 29, 32, 35, 35) sts of chart once more. Work Rows 2–16 of Scrollwork chart, and *at the same time* inc 1 st at neck edge (beg of WS rows; end of RS rows) 4 times, then use the cable method to CO 2 sts at neck edge at beg of next 5 WS rows, working new sts into patt from chart—89 (89, 93, 96, 99, 99) sts. *Next row:* (RS) With light brown, *k5 (5, 5, 5, 4, 4), k2tog; rep from * 6 (6, 7, 7, 9, 9) more times, k40 (40, 37, 40, 39, 39)—82 (82, 85, 88, 89, 89) sts rem. *Next row:* (WS) With light brown, CO 0 (0, 2, 1, 2, 2) st(s) at neck edge, knit to end—82 (82, 87, 89, 91, 91) sts. *Next row:* (RS) With light brown, knit. *Next row:* (WS) With light brown, CO 0 (0, 2, 4, 0, 2) sts at neck edge, knit to end—82 (82, 89, 93, 91, 93) sts. *Next row:* (RS) Change to olive and work horizontal I-cord. *Next row:* (WS) With olive, CO 0 (0, 0, 0, 5, 7) sts at neck edge, knit to end—82 (82, 89, 93, 96, 100) sts.

Shape Armhole

Row 1: (RS) With plum, ssk, *k4 (4, 4, 4, 3, 3), k2tog; rep from * 6 (6, 7, 7, 8, 8) more times, k38 (38, 39, 43, 49, 53)—74 (74, 80, 84, 86, 90) sts rem.

Row 2: With plum, knit to last 3 sts, ssk, k1—73 (73, 79, 83, 85, 89) sts.

Row 3: With plum, ssk, *k3 (3, 3, 3, 2, 2), ssk; rep from * 6 (6, 7, 7, 8, 8) more times, k36 (36, 37, 41, 47, 51)—65 (65, 70, 74, 75, 79) sts rem.

Rows 4 and 6: (WS) With plum, purl to last 3 sts, ssp, p1—1 st dec'd at armhole edge each row.

Row 5: With plum, ssk, *k2 (2, 2, 2, 1, 1), ssk; rep from * 6 (6, 7, 7, 8, 8) more times, k34 (34, 35, 39, 45, 49)—56 (56, 60, 64, 64, 68) sts rem.

Row 7: With plum, ssk, *k1 (1, 1, 1, 0, 0), ssk; rep from * 6 (6, 7, 7, 8, 8) more times, k32 (32, 33, 37, 43, 47)—47 (47, 50, 54, 53, 57) sts rem.

Embroidery

⊙◎ French Knot

🌾 Chain Stitch

Row 8: With plum, purl to last 3 sts, ssp, p1—1 st dec'd.

Row 9: With plum, ssk, knit to end—1 st dec'd.

Rows 10 and 11: Rep Rows 8 and 9—43 (43, 46, 50, 49, 53) sts rem.

Cont with plum, work short-rows as foll:

Row 12: (WS) P15, wrap next st, turn.

Row 13: Knit to end.

Row 14: Purl to 2 sts before previous wrapped st, wrap next st, turn.

Rows 15–26: Rep the last 2 rows 6 more times—last wrapped st is the 2nd st in from shoulder edge (end of RS rows).

Row 27: Knit to end.

Row 28: Purl across all sts, working wrapped sts tog with their wraps.

Cont even in St st with plum until shoulder selvedge (end of RS rows) measures 3¾ (4¾, 5½, 6¼, 7, 7¾)" (9.5 [12, 14, 16, 18, 19.5] cm) from last sts CO at neck edge, or same as left back shoulder, ending with a WS row. Place sts on holder.

FINISHING

Steam block all pieces, transferring held sts from holders to waste yarn if necessary.

Embroidery

With plum, work French knots (see pages 148 and 149, for embroidery stitches) on right front and back where shown on Flower chart. With olive, work lines of chain-stitch embroidery on the lower body and left front following the purl sts of Scrollwork chart as shown in diagram above. Work clusters of French knots using yellow-green and plum in scrollwork sections as shown on diagram.

With yarn threaded on a tapestry needle, sew shoulder seams. Sew left side seam, easing selvedge of left front to fit.

Left Armhole Edging

Place 43 (43, 46, 50, 49, 53) held sts of left front on shorter cir needle and join light brown with RS facing. Knit across sts on needle, dec 2 (2, 5, 6, 6, 10) sts evenly spaced as you go, pick up and knit 40 (43, 45, 46, 50, 54) sts along back armhole edge, pm, and join for working in the rnd—81 (84, 86, 90, 93, 97) sts total. With light brown, knit 1 rnd, then purl 1 rnd. With plum, knit 1 rnd, then purl 1 rnd. With yellow-green, knit 1 rnd, then purl 1 rnd. With olive, work I-cord BO (see Stitch Guide).

Right Armhole Edging

With shorter cir needle, light brown, and beg at base of armhole, pick up and knit 81 (84, 86, 90, 93, 97) sts evenly spaced around armhole edge, pm, and join for working in the rnd. Work as for left armhole edging.

Lower Border

Carefully remove waste yarn from provisional CO and place 175 (200, 225, 250, 275, 300) live sts on longer cir needle. Pm and join for working in the rnd. With light brown, knit 1 rnd, then purl 1 rnd. With plum, knit 1 rnd, then purl 1 rnd. With yellow-green, knit 1 rnd, then purl 1 rnd. With olive, work I-cord BO.

Collar

With olive, shorter cir needle, RS facing, and beg at center front neck, pick up and knit 60 (65, 70, 75, 80, 90) sts evenly spaced around neck opening. Do not join. *Next row:* (WS) With olive, knit. *Next row:* (RS) With olive, work horizontal I-cord. *Next row:* (WS) With olive, knit. Place 3 sts at each end of row on holder—54 (59, 64, 69, 74, 84) sts. Change to light brown and work short-rows to shape front edges of collar as foll:

Rows 1 and 2: Knit to last 3 sts, wrap next st, turn.

Rows 3 and 4: Knit to 1 st before previous wrapped st, wrap next st, turn.

Rows 5–10: Rep Rows 3 and 4 three more times—collar measures about 1¼" (3.2 cm) from upper edge of horizontal I-cord.

Break yarn. Return 3 held sts at right front neck to shorter cir needle with RS facing and join olive. *Next row:* With olive, *k2, ssk; return 3 sts just worked to left needle; bring yarn around the back of the I-cord in position to work a RS row again; rep from * until only 3 I-cord sts rem and all light brown collar sts have been joined. With yarn threaded on a tapestry needle, graft 3 rem sts to 3 held sts at left front neck.

Button Loop

With olive, make a 6" (15 cm) twisted-cord loop (see page 150). Sew loop to right front neck opening at base of light brown section of collar. Sew button to left front opposite button loop; button shown is a custom crocheted button made with plum.

Weave in loose ends. Block lightly again to measurements.

TRIBAL BABY CARRIER
LISA B. EVANS

In many cultures, mothers "wear" their babies as they go about their daily tasks. **Lisa B. Evans** created a colorful knitted version of what is traditionally constructed in woven fabric, taking inspiration from Middle Eastern kilim rugs and African kente cloth. She worked a kaleidoscope of warm colors in a combination of stripes, intarsia, and subtly textured linen stitch to give the rich look of antique textiles. The fabric lining, a batik cotton cloth in complementary colors, adds another layer of cultural tradition.

STITCH GUIDE

Linen Stitch (even number of sts):
Row 1: Sl 1 kwise with yarn in back (wyb), *sl 1 pwise with yarn in front (wyf), k1; rep from * to last st, k1.
Row 2: Sl 1 kwise wyb, *sl 1 pwise wyb, p1; rep from * to last st, k1.
Repeat Rows 1 and 2 for pattern.

Ribbed Linen Stitch (even number of sts):
Row 1: (RS) Sl 1 kwise wyb, *slip 1 pwise wyf, k1, rep from * to last st, k1.
Row 2: (WS) Sl 1 kwise wyb, purl to last st, k1
Repeat Rows 1 and 2 for pattern.

BODY

Center Section

With crochet hook and waste yarn, use the chain crochet provisional method (see Glossary, page 153) to CO 77 sts onto cir needle. With RS facing, join red. Work Rows 1–135 of Diamonds chart, using a separate length of yarn for each color block (see Notes, page 82)—piece measures about 25" (63.5 cm) from CO. Set aside.

Left Edging

With crochet hook and waste yarn, use the crochet provisional method to CO 24 sts onto straight needle. Join caramel with RS facing. Using straight needle or dpn as desired, work in linen st (see Stitch Guide) changing colors as foll (see Notes): 13 rows caramel, 1 row red, 2

YARN
Worsted weight (#4 Medium).

Shown here: Nashua Handknits Creative Focus Cotton (100% mercerized cotton; 93 yd [85 m]/50 g): #29 caramel, 5 skeins; #10 passion (red), #07 copper, and #31 black, 4 skeins each; #13 pettit purple and #28 beige, 3 skeins each; #22 grass green, 2 skeins; #26 sage, 1 skein. Yarn is used double throughout.

NEEDLES
Size 7 (4.5 mm): straight, set of 5 double-pointed (dpn), and 32" (80 cm) circular (cir). Adjust needle size if necessary to obtain the correct gauge.

NOTIONS
Size H/8 (4.75 mm) crochet hook and waste yarn for provisional cast-on; stitch holders; tapestry needle; pins; 1 yd (0.9 meter) of 45" (114 cm) lining fabric (use an old scarf or sarong, if desired); sharp-point sewing needle and matching thread for attaching lining; two wooden or decorative plastic rings with 4" (10 cm) diameter opening (available at fabric and craft stores).

GAUGE
18 stitches and 21½ rows = 4" (10 cm) in stockinette-stitch intarsia patt from Diamonds chart using a double strand of yarn; 17½" stitches and 33 stitches = 4" (10 cm) in linen-stitch patt using a double strand of yarn.

❖ This project is worked using a doubled strand of yarn throughout. If only a single ball of yarn is available for a particular color, work holding the ends from the inside and outside of same ball together.

❖ Work the charted pattern in stockinette-stitch intarsia, using separate lengths of yarn for each color section, and twisting yarns together at color changes to avoid leaving holes. Do not strand the unused colors across the back side of the work.

❖ To make the knitting manageable, work with cut lengths of yarn—each about as long as both of your arms outstretched. To reduce the amount of finishing, weave in the ends as you go.

❖ When working the edging pieces, if a color will be used again within four rows, it is not necessary to cut strands between color changes. Carry the unused color along the side of the work up to where it is needed next, catching it against the selvedge by twisting it together with the working color.

❖ The top and bottom edges of the body are folded into pleats, which are secured by working stitches together across the top of each pleat. The straps are worked outward from the ends of the pleated sections, with an extra pleat worked near the beginning of each strap to narrow the strap further.

❖ This baby carrier is sized for an average-size person and may be adjusted by tightening or loosening the strap at the ring closure. The carrier should initially fit very snugly because it will stretch out over time. Once the strap is adjusted to your satisfaction, you can maintain the same fit by taking the carrier on and off over your head to avoid changing the strap position.

rows green, 1 row red, 1 row black, 2 rows beige, 1 row black, 4 rows copper, 1 row black, 2 rows beige, 1 row black, 1 row red, 2 rows green, 1 row red. Cont in linen st, rep the color sequence of the last 33 rows 5 more times—piece measures about 23½" to 24½" (59.5 to 62 cm) from CO when slightly stretched. (*Note:* Because there are an odd number of rows in the color sequence and the pattern is worked over 2 rows, the first color sequence will begin on a RS row, but thereafter the color sequence will alternate between starting on a WS or RS row.) With caramel only, work even in linen st until piece measures 25" (63.5 cm) from CO when slightly stretched, ending with a WS row. With RS of both center and edging facing, transfer edging sts to end of cir needle holding center sts; edging should be on the left side of the center section, at the end of the center's RS rows—101 sts total on cir. Align CO edges of both pieces and use the mattress st (see Glossary, page 156) and single strand of yarn threaded on a tapestry needle to seam the edging and center tog, easing in any fullness.

Right Edging

With crochet hook and waste yarn, use the crochet provisional method to CO 24 sts onto straight needle. Join caramel with RS facing. Using straight needle or dpn as desired, work in linen st changing colors as foll: 13 rows caramel, 1 row red, 2 rows purple, 1 row red, 1 row black, 2 rows beige, 1 row black, 4 rows green, 1 row black, 2 rows beige, 1 row black, 1 row red, 2 rows purple, 1 row red. Cont in linen st, rep the color sequence of the last 33 rows 5 more times—piece measures about 23½" to 24½" (59.5 to 62 cm) from CO when slightly stretched. With caramel only, work even in linen st until piece measures 25" (63.5 cm) from CO when slightly stretched, ending with a WS row. Place sts on holder. Turn piece upside down so provisional CO is at the top; this is done deliberately so the stripes of the two edging pieces will be offset for visual interest. Carefully release edging sts from provisional CO, and with RS of both edging and body facing, transfer edging sts to beg of cir needle holding body sts; edging should be on the right side of the center section, at the beg of the center's RS rows—125 sts total on cir needle. Align lower edges of both pieces and use the mattress st and single strand of yarn threaded on a tapestry needle to seam the edging and body tog, easing in any fullness. Assembled body piece measures about 28" (71 cm) wide and 25" (63.5 cm) high.

FIRST PLEATED SECTION AND SHORT STRAP

With RS facing, rejoin copper to beg of assembled body sts on cir needle—125 sts. Work 2 rows as foll, ending with a WS row: Work 24 sts in linen st, 77 center sts in St st, 24 sts in linen st.

Pleat Row 1

(RS) K29, sl next 11 sts onto dpn, then sl foll 11 sts onto another dpn. Fold second dpn to front, parallel to first dpn, with RS of fabric on each dpn touching. Make another fold to bring next 11 sts on cir needle parallel to sts on both dpn, with sts on cir needle in front of both dpn.

Work k3tog (1 st from cir and 1 st from each dpn tog) 11 times, k1—41 sts on right needle; 62 sts unworked on left needle. Sl next 11 sts onto dpn, then slip foll 11 sts onto another dpn. Fold second dpn to back, parallel with first dpn, with WS of fabric on each needle touching. Make another fold to bring the next 11 sts on cir needle parallel to sts on both dpn, with sts on cir needle in back of both dpn. Work k3tog (1 st from cir needle and 1 st from each dpn tog) 11 times, k29—81 sts rem. Work 1 WS row as sl 1 kwise wyb, purl to last st, k1. Break yarn.

Pleat Row 2

(RS) Place first 14 sts on dpn and fold dpn to back of work, parallel to cir needle, with WS of fabric on each needle touching, and sts on cir needle in front. Rejoin copper with RS facing to sts on cir needle, then work k2tog (1 st from cir needle tog with 1 st from dpn) 14 times, k12, k2tog, k11—38 sts on right needle; 28 unworked sts on left needle. Sl next 14 sts onto dpn, then sl rem 14 sts onto another dpn. Fold second dpn to back, with WS of fabric on each needle touching, and first dpn in front. Work k2tog (1 st from each dpn tog) 14 times—52 sts rem.

Change to purple, and purl 1 WS row across all sts.

▨	caramel
◒	red
✕	copper
▦	black
◇	purple
·	beige
+	green
−	sage

Diamonds

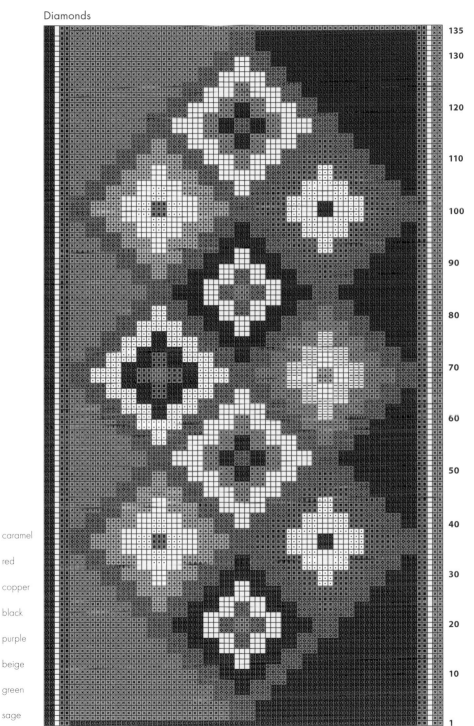

Combine color and texture for the rich look of antique textiles.

Strap

Work in ribbed linen st (see Stitch Guide), changing colors as foll:

Rows 1–5: With purple, work 5 rows.

Rows 6 and 7: With red, work 2 rows.

Rows 8–11: With green, work 4 rows, ending with Row 1 of linen st patt.

Rnd 12: With RS facing, arrange sts evenly on 4 dpn (13 sts on each needle), and join for working in the rnd. With black and RS still facing, *sl 1 pwise wyf, k1; rep from * to end. (*Note:* Rnds 12–15 are all worked as RS rnds.)

Rnd 13: With black, *k1, sl 1 pwise wyf; rep from * to end.

Rnd 14: With black, work as for Rnd 12.

Rnd 15: (pleat rnd) Break yarn. Fold first 2 dpn tog with WS of fabric on each needle touching and sts on second dpn of rnd in front. Rejoin black with RS facing to sts on second dpn, then work k2tog (1 st from each dpn tog) 13 times. Fold the 2 rem dpn tog with WS of fabric on each needle touching and third dpn of rnd in front. Work k2tog (1 st from each dpn tog) 13 times—26 sts rem.

Row 16: (WS) Place all sts on one dpn or straight needle with WS facing in preparation for working back and forth in rows again. With black, sl 1 kwise wyb, purl to last st, k1.

Rows 17–44: Work 28 rows in black in ribbed linen st, ending with a WS row.

Rows 45 and 46: With green, sl 1 kwise wyb, *p1, k1; rep from * to last st, k1.

Row 47: Beg with this row, the ribbed linen st patt reverses so the WS of the patt corresponds to the RS of the strap; this is so the RS of the patt will show when strap is passed through the rings and folded back to fasten. With green, sl 1 kwise wyb, *sl 1 pwise wyb, p1; rep from * to last st, k1.

Row 48: (WS of strap, RS of reversed patt) With green, sl 1 kwise wyb, knit to end.

Row 49: (RS of strap, WS of reversed patt) With green, sl 1 kwise wyb, *sl 1 pwise wyb, p1; rep from * to last st, k1.

Rows 50–84: Rep the patt of Rows 48 and 49 seventeen more times, then work Row 48 once more, changing colors as foll: 2 rows caramel, 4 rows purple, 22 rows copper, 5 rows beige, 2 rows green.

Row 85: With black, sl 1 kwise wyb, *sl 1 pwise wyb, p1; rep from * to last st, k1.

Row 86: With black, k2tog, knit to last 2 sts, k2tog—2 sts dec'd.

Rows 87 and 88: Rep Rows 85 and 86.

Rows 89–100: With red, rep Rows 85 and 86 six more times—12 sts rem; strap measures about 11½" (29 cm) from beg of ribbed linen st patt.

BO all sts kwise with red.

SECOND PLEATED SECTION AND LONG STRAP

Carefully remove provisional CO from base of center and left edging, place sts on cir needle, then transfer live sts of right edging from holder to cir needle—125 sts. With RS facing, join red to beg of sts on needle and with red work as for first pleated section until Pleat Row 2 has been completed—52 sts rem.

Change to beige and purl 1 WS row across all sts.

Strap

Work in ribbed linen st, changing colors as foll:

Rows 1–5: With beige, work 5 rows.

Rows 6 and 7: With green, work 2 rows.

Rows 8–11: With black, work 4 rows.

Rnds 12–15: With caramel, work as for Rnds 12–15 of first pleated section—26 sts rem.

Row 16: (WS) With caramel, work as for Row 16 of first pleated section.

Rows 17–226: Cont in ribbed linen st, changing colors as foll: 17 rows caramel, 5 rows red, 2 rows copper, 4 rows purple, 22 rows caramel, 5 rows green, 2 rows beige, 4 rows copper, 22 rows caramel, 5 rows beige, 2 rows green, 4 rows black, 22 rows copper, 5 rows red, 2 rows caramel, 4 rows purple, 22 rows copper, 5 rows green, 2 rows beige, 4 rows caramel, 50 rows copper—strap measures about 26" (66 cm) from beg of ribbed linen st patt.

Transfer sts to dpn if you are not already working on a dpn and cut yarn, leaving a long tail. With rings held tog, sl dpn holding live sts through both rings. Fold end of strap down about 1½" (3.8 cm) on WS to enclose rings. Using tail threaded on a tapestry needle, sew live sts to WS of strap, carefully following a single row of sts to keep the sewing line straight.

FINISHING

Weave in all ends.

Lining

Cut a piece of lining fabric about 19" (48.5 cm) wide and 26" (63.5 cm) high. (*Note:* For extra support, use a double layer of lining fabric.) Turn all 4 edges of lining ½" (1.3 cm) to WS and press in place. Lay carrier on flat surface with WS of body facing up. Fold the selvedge of each edging about 2½" (6.5 cm) to WS along its entire length and pin in place—with sides folded in, body measures about 23" (58.5 cm) wide from one folded edge to the other. With sewing needle and thread and WS of carrier still facing, sew long sides of lining to selvedges of edgings. Fold the short sides of the lining into pleats to match the width of the pleated carrier body and sew across each short side of lining to secure pleats.

To wear, pass end of short strap through both rings, then back in the opposite direction through only one ring as shown. Put carrier on over your head and adjust straps to where best fit is achieved.

The inspiration for this playful pullover was the traditional six-point star motif used in Scandinavian designs. Using graph paper, **Ann Budd** blew up a single star motif to fill the entire front of a sweater. To break from tradition, she used a contemporary cropped pullover shape with stand-up collar and worked it in a bulkier-than-expected yarn in the unconventional color combination of burnt orange and burgundy. For a bit of finishing detail, the cuffs and lower body are trimmed with a clean hem with a picot edge.

BACK

With MC and smaller straight needles, CO 60 (68) sts. Beg and end with a WS row and knitting the first and last st of every row for garter st selvedges, work center 58 (66) sts even in St st (knit RS rows; purl WS rows) for 7 rows for facing. *Picot row:* (RS) K1, *yo, k2tog; rep from * to last st, k1. Cont working garter st selvedges, work even in St st for 7 more rows. *Join hem.* Using the single needle 3 or 4 sizes smaller than main needles, slip the single needle into each st of CO to pick up 60 (68) sts; these sts are just picked up and placed on the needle without being worked (do not pick up and knit them). Fold hem in half along the picot row to bring the two needles tog with RS of fabric facing outwards, and needle with picked-up sts in back of needle with live sts. Holding both needles tog in the left hand, *k2tog to join 1 live st tog with 1 picked up st; rep from * to end—still 60 (68) sts. Change to larger needles. Cont garter st selvedges, work even in St st until piece measures 5 (6)" (12.5 [15] cm) from picot row, ending with a WS row.

Shape Armholes

BO 3 sts at beg of next 4 rows—48 (56) sts rem. Dec 1 st each end of needle every RS row 1 (2) time(s)—46 (52) sts rem. Cont garter st selvedges, work even in St st until armholes measure 7 (7½)" (18 [19] cm), ending with a WS row.

Shape Shoulders

BO 6 sts at beg of next 2 (4) rows, then BO 5 sts at beg of foll 2 (0) rows—24 (28) sts rem. BO all sts.

FRONT

With MC, CO 60 (68) sts and work as for back until piece measures 2½ (3½)" (6.5 [9] cm) from picot row, ending with a WS row, and placing markers (pm) on each side of center 34

FINISHED SIZE

28 (32)" (71 [81.5] cm) chest/bust circumference. Sweater shown measures 32" (81.5 cm).

YARN

Worsted weight (#4 Medium).

Shown here: Classic Elite Bazic Wool (100% superwash wool; 65 yd [59 m]/ 50 g). #2958 barn red (MC) 8 (9) balls and #2985 marigold (orange, CC),1 ball.

NEEDLES

Body and sleeves—size 9 (5.5 mm): straight and 16" (40 cm) circular (cir). Hem and collar—size 8 (5 mm): straight and 16" (40 cm) cir. Adjust needle size if necessary to obtain the correct gauge.

NOTIONS

One needle 3 or 4 sizes smaller than main needles for joining hem facings; markers (m); tapestry needle.

GAUGE

17 stitches and 24 rows = 4" (10 cm) in stockinette stitch.

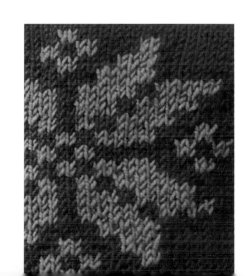

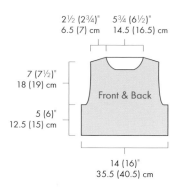

Front & Back

2½ (2¾)"
6.5 (7) cm

5¾ (6½)"
14.5 (16.5) cm

7 (7½)"
18 (19) cm

5 (6)"
12.5 (15) cm

14 (16)"
35.5 (40.5) cm

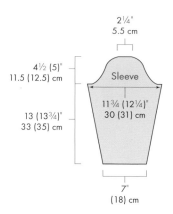

Sleeve

2¼"
5.5 cm

4½ (5)"
11.5 (12.5) cm

13 (13¾)"
33 (35) cm

11¾ (12¼)"
30 (31) cm

7"
(18) cm

sts to mark patt section on the last row—13 (17) sts outside markers at each end of row. *Next row:* (RS) Cont in St st with MC on sts at each side of center, join CC and work Row 1 of Star chart over marked center 34 sts. *Note:* Star chart will still be in progress when armhole shaping begins; read the next section all the way through before proceeding. Cont garter st selvedges, work Rows 2–34 of Star chart, and *at the same time,* when piece measures 5 (6)" (12.5 [15 cm) from picot row, shape armholes as for back—46 (52) sts rem; 6 (9) sts outside markers at each end of row. When chart has been completed, cont even in St st with MC until armholes measure 5½ (5¾)" (14 [14.5] cm), ending with a WS row.

Shape Neck

(RS) Keeping in patt, work 16 (18) sts, join new ball of MC and BO next 14 (16) sts, work to end—16 (18) sts each side. Working each side separately, at each neck edge BO 2 (3) sts once, then dec 1 st every RS row 3 times—11 (12) sts rem each side. Cont even until armholes measure 7 (7½)" (18 [19] cm).

Shape Shoulders

At each armhole edge, BO 6 sts once, then BO rem 5 (6) sts.

SLEEVES

With MC and smaller straight needles, CO 30 sts for both sizes. Beg and end with a WS row and knitting the first and last st of every row for garter st selvedges, work center 28 sts in St st for 5 rows for facing. Work picot row as for back, then work 5 more rows in St st, ending with a WS row. Join hem as for back. Change to larger needles and purl 1 row WS row. *Next row:* (RS) Knit, inc 1 st each end of needle—32 sts. Cont garter st selvedges, work St st for 3 more rows. *Next row:* (RS) Join CC and work Row 1 of Sleeve chart. *Note:* Sleeve chart will still be in progress during sleeve shaping; read the next section all the way through before proceeding. Cont garter st selvedges, work Rows 2–6 of Sleeve chart, and *at the same time* inc 1 st each end of needle every 4th row once, then every 6th row 8 (9) times, working new

Star

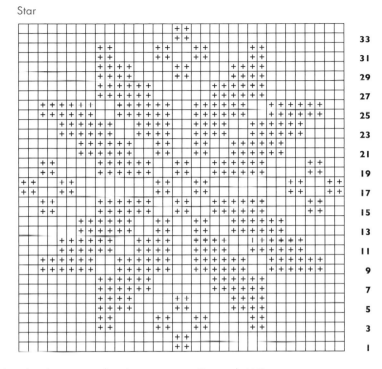

Sleeve

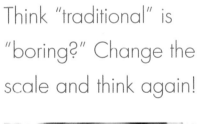

Legend:
- ☐ St st with MC
- ✚ St st with CC
- ▢ pattern repeat

sts in St st with MC—50 (52) sts. When chart has been completed, cont even in St st with MC and garter st selvedges until piece measures 13 (13¾)" (33 [35] cm) from picot row, ending with a WS row.

Shape Cap

BO 3 sts at beg of next 4 rows—38 (40) sts rem. Dec 1 st each end of needle every RS row 10 (11) times—18 sts rem for both sizes. BO 4 (2) sts at beg of next 2 (4) rows—10 sts rem. BO all sts.

FINISHING

Weave in loose ends. Block pieces to measurements. With yarn threaded on a tapestry needle, sew shoulder seams. Sew sleeve caps into armholes. Sew sleeve and side seams.

Collar

With MC, larger cir needle, RS facing, and beg at right shoulder seam, pick up and knit 24 (28) sts across back neck, 12 (13) sts along left front neck edge, 14 (16) sts across front neck, 12 (13) sts along right front neck edge—62 (70) sts total. Pm and join for working in the rnd. Work even in St st (knit every rnd) until piece measures 2" (5 cm) from pick-up rnd. Work picot row as for back. Change to smaller cir needle and work even in St st until piece measures 2" (5 cm) from picot row for facing. Loosely BO all sts. Turn facing to WS along picot row, and with yarn threaded on a tapestry needle, sew BO edge to pick-up rnd at base of collar. Lightly steam-block seams.

Think "traditional" is "boring?" Change the scale and think again!

Inspired by crewelwork found on traditional fabrics from India, **Gayle Bunn** artfully played with proportion and exploded large felted flowers and leaves onto a truly modern skirt. Gayle felted knitted strips of fabric, then cut out the flower and leaf motifs to appliqué onto six unfelted skirt panels. Finally, she joined the motifs with embroidered chain-stitched vines. Gayle chose a folk-art palette of a warm red worked with faded shades of cool blue and olive that evokes the look of aged tapestry.

SKIRT PANEL (MAKE 6)

With MC and straight needles, CO 50 (52, 54) sts. Beg with a RS row, work in St st (knit on RS; purl on WS) until piece measures 1½" (3.8 cm) from CO, ending with a WS row. *Dec row:* K1, k2tog, knit to last 3 sts, ssk (see Glossary, page 154), k1—2 sts dec'd. Work 9 rows even in St st. Cont in St st, rep the shaping of the last 10 rows 7 more times—34 (36, 38) sts rem. Rep Dec row—2 sts dec'd. Work 13 rows even in St st. Cont in St st, rep the shaping of the last 14 rows 1 more time, then rep Dec row once more—28 (30, 32) sts rem; piece measures about 17" (43 cm) from CO measured straight up along a single column of sts; do not measure along shaped selvedges. Cont even until piece measures 24" (61 cm) from CO, ending with a WS row. *Note:* To adjust finished length, work more or fewer rows here; every 7 rows added or removed will lengthen or shorten the skirt by 1" (2.5 cm) and will alter the placement of the embroidery. BO all sts. Make 5 more skirt panels in the same manner.

EMBROIDERY

With wax pencil, mark curved line for vine on each panel as shown on embroidery diagram, with the lower end of each vine about 1" (2.5 cm) above CO edge, and the upper end of each vine about 1" (2.5 cm) below BO edge. With espresso threaded on a tapestry needle, work chain stitch embroidery (see page 148) along all vine lines.

FELTED FABRIC FOR LEAVES
(MAKE 1 EACH WITH BLUE PINE AND KHAKI)

With straight needles, CO 48 sts. Work even in St st until piece measures 29" (73.5 cm) from CO. Loosely BO all sts.

FINISHED SIZE

About 34½ (36, 39)" (87.5 [91.5, 99] cm) hip circumference measured 7" (18 cm) below top edge of skirt, and 24" (61 cm) long for all sizes. Skirt shown measures 34½" (87.5 cm).

YARN

Worsted weight (#4 Medium).

Shown here: Nashua Handknits Creative Focus Worsted (75% wool, 25% alpaca; 220 yd [201 m]/100 g): #2055 carmine (MC, red), 5 (6, 7) balls; #1450 blue pine, #4899 khaki (green), #0100 natural, #2190 copper, and #0410 espresso (dark brown), 1 ball each.

NEEDLES

Size 7 (4.5 mm): straight and 36" (90 cm) circular (cir). Adjust needle size if necessary to obtain the correct gauge.

NOTIONS

Tapestry needle; stitch marker (m); sewing pins; wax pencil or dressmaker's marking pencil for drawing embroidery details on skirt and cutting lines on felted pieces; thin cardboard for cutting templates; ¾" (2 cm) wide elastic in length to fit around wearer's hips 2" (5 cm) below waist; ¾ yd [0.7 meter] of 54" (137 cm) wide lining fabric; sewing machine; sharp-point sewing needle and thread to match lining fabric; four ⅝" (1.5 cm) buttons.

GAUGE

20 stitches and 28 rows = 4" (10 cm) in stockinette stitch.

FELTED FABRIC FOR FLOWERS
(MAKE 1 EACH WITH COPPER AND NATURAL)

With straight needles, CO 34 sts. Work even in St st until piece measures 29" (73.5 cm) from CO. Loosely BO all sts.

FELTING

Weave in all loose ends. Set washing machine at lowest water level (enough to just cover the fabric pieces), hottest temperature, and highest agitation. Place blue pine, khaki, and copper pieces (not the natural pieces, which might pick up loose fibers from the other colors) in washer with an old pair of jeans for extra agitation and small amount of liquid detergent. Do *not* felt the skirt panels. Begin wash cycle and check felting progress every 5 minutes until fabric is firm and individual sts are no longer easily visible. Remove pieces and rinse by hand in lukewarm water. Roll pieces in towels to remove excess water. Repeat for the natural pieces seperately. Lay flat and air-dry completely.

APPLIQUÉ

Transfer leaf and flower shapes shown at right onto thin cardboard, and carefully cut out each cardboard template. Using the cardboard templates, trace the following number and types of shapes onto felted fabric pieces:

Large Leaf: 12 khaki, 6 blue pine
Medium Leaf: 12 khaki, 18 blue pine
Small Leaf: 18 khaki, 18 blue pine
Large Flower: 3 copper, 3 natural
Small Flower: 3 copper, 3 natural
Large Flower Center: 3 copper, 3 natural
Small Flower Center: 3 copper, 3 natural.

Using matching yarn threaded on tapestry needle, sew a contrasting flower center in the middle of each flower. Following diagram at right, position leaves and flowers along embroidered vine on each skirt panel, alternating flower colors as shown in photograph, and pin in place. With matching yarn threaded on tapestry needle, sew all the way around each felted piece to secure.

LINING

Using one skirt panel as a guide, cut out 6 lining pieces, adding ½" (1.3 cm) seam allowances along each side, and cutting top and bottom edges of lining even with BO and CO edges of skirt panel so lining will be shorter than skirt when finished. With sewing machine and matching thread, sew lining panels tog at sides, leaving top 6" (15 cm) of left side seam open. Fold lining hem up 1" (2.5 cm), press, and sew in place.

5¾ (6, 6½)"
14.5 (15, 16.5) cm

7"
18 cm

17"
43 cm

One Panel

10 (10½, 10¾)"
25.5 (26.5, 27.5) cm

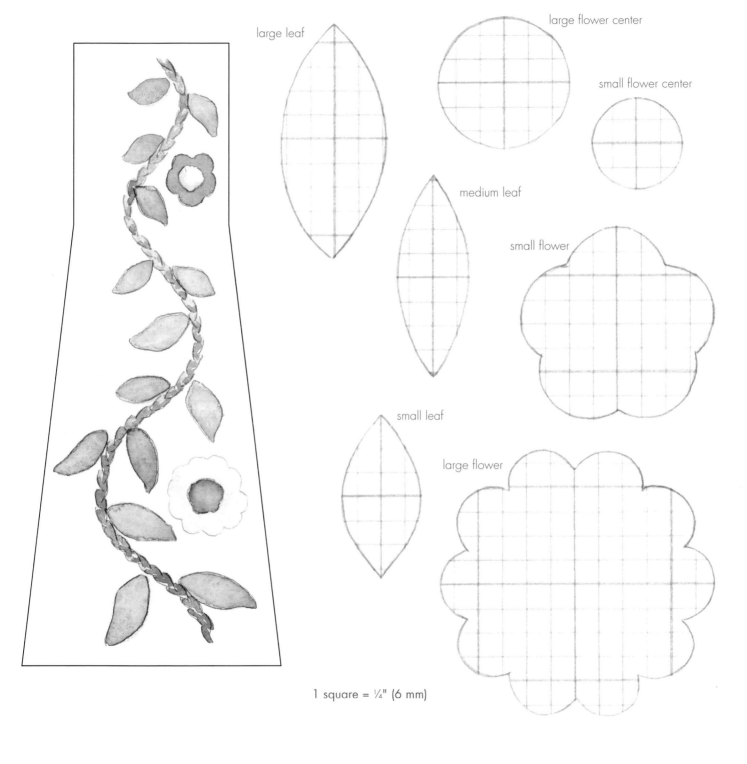

large leaf

large flower center

small flower center

medium leaf

small flower

small leaf

large flower

1 square = ¼" (6 mm)

FINISHING

Weave in loose ends. Block skirt panels to measurements. With yarn threaded on a tapestry needle, sew panels tog, alternating flower colors as shown and leaving top 6" (15 cm) of left side seam open.

Waistband Facing

With MC, RS facing, cir needle, and beg at top of left side opening, pick up and knit 25 (27, 29) sts across BO edge at top of each panel—150 (162, 174) sts total. Do not join. Working back and forth in rows, knit 1 WS row for fold line, then beg with a RS (knit) row, work 6 rows St st. Loosely BO all sts.

Buttonband

With MC, RS facing, straight needles, and beg at waistband fold line, pick up and knit 30 sts along back edge of left side opening to top of seam. Work in garter st for 4 rows. With WS facing, BO all sts kwise.

Buttonhole Band

With MC, RS facing, straight needles, and beg at top of seam, pick up and knit 30 sts along front edge of left side opening to waistband fold line. *Buttonhole row:* (WS) K2, *BO 2 sts, k5 (6 sts on right needle after buttonhole gap); rep from * 2 more times, BO 2 sts, knit to end. *Next row:* (RS) Knit, and *at the same time* use the backward-loop method (see Glossary, page 152) to CO 2 sts over each gap in previous row to complete buttonholes. With WS facing, BO all sts kwise.

Hem

With MC, RS facing, cir needle, and beg at left side seam, pick up and knit 49 (51, 53) sts across bottom of each panel—294 (306, 318) sts total. Place marker (pm) and join for working in the rnd. Purl 1 rnd for fold line. Knit 6 rnds. Loosely BO all sts.

Fold hem and waistband facing to WS along fold lines and sew in place using MC threaded on tapestry needle, leaving selvedges of waistband facing open. Cut elastic to fit comfortably about 2" (5 cm) below natural waistline. Thread elastic through waistband facing and pin ends of elastic even with pick-up rows of button and buttonhole bands. Try skirt on and adjust elastic length if necessary. Using sewing needle and thread, stitch ends of elastic securely to skirt on WS. Sew buttons to back edge of left side opening, opposite buttonholes. Turn edges along top and side opening of lining ½" (1.3 cm) to WS and press. Pin folded top edge of lining even with BO edge of waistband facing, matching side openings. With sewing needle and thread, sew lining in place by hand on WS of skirt across top edge and along side opening.

A visit
Tom To
of autu
reds of
individu
of Can
combin

LEG
With MC
for worki
Rnd 1: *
Rnds 2–7
With A,

Child's si
dec 3 sts
with MC
6¾" (17 c

Woman's
MC dec
once mor
(20.5 cm)

HEEL
Slip last 1
needle—2
these sts e

Less is more . . .
but sometimes more
is better.

Woman's Sock

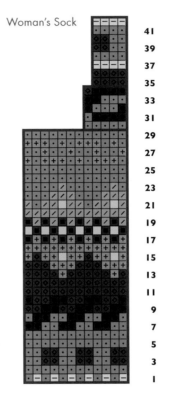

41 39 37 35 33 31 29 27 25 23 21 19 17 15 13 11 9 7 5 3 1

Child's Sock

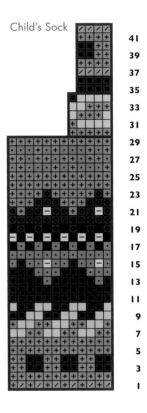

41 39 37 35 33 31 29 27 25 23 21 19 17 15 13 11 9 7 5 3 1

green	+ medium blue
− gold	• orange
⟋ purple	◈ red

● burgundy
■ navy
☐ pattern repeat

Color play—think of it as finger-painting for grownups.

Heel Flap

Work 24 (28) heel sts back and forth in rows as foll:

Row 1: (RS) *K1, sl 1 as if to purl with yarn in back (pwise wyb); rep from * to last 2 sts, k2.

Row 2: Purl.

Rep Rows 1 and 2 rows until heel measures 1¾ (2)" (4.5 [5] cm), ending with a WS row.

Turn Heel

Work short-rows as foll:

Row 1: (RS) K14 (16), ssk, k1, turn work.

Row 2: (WS) Sl 1 pwise with yarn in front (wyf), p5, p2tog, p1, turn.

Row 3: Sl 1 pwise wyb, knit to 1 st before gap made on previous row, ssk (1 st from each side of gap), k1, turn.

Row 4: Sl 1 pwise wyf, purl to 1 st before gap made on previous row, p2tog (1 st from each side of gap), p1, turn.

Rep Rows 3 and 4 until all heel sts have been worked, ending with a WS row and ending the last rep with ssk on Row 3, and p2tog on Row 4, if there are not enough sts to work the final k1 or p1 after the dec—14 (16) sts rem.

Shape Gusset

With MC and RS facing, knit across heel sts, then with the same needle (Needle 1) pick up and knit 13 (15) sts along selvedge of heel flap; with Needle 2, k24 (28) instep sts; with Needle 3, pick up and knit 13 (15) sts along other selvedge of heel flap, then knit the first 7 (8) heel sts from Needle 1 again—64 (74) sts total; 20 (23) sts each on Needle 1 and Needle 3, 24 (28) sts on Needle 2. Rnd begins at center back heel.

Rnd 2: On Needle 1, knit to last 3 sts, k2tog, k1; on Needle 2, knit; on Needle 3, k1, ssk, knit to end—2 sts dec'd.

Rnd 3: Knit.

Rep Rnds 2 and 3 seven (eight) more times—48 (56) sts rem; 12 (14) sts each on Needle 1 and Needle 3, 24 (28) sts on Needle 2.

FOOT

Working according to chart for your size, work Rnds 37–42 once, then rep Rnds 35–42 two (three) times. With MC, knit 1 rnd—foot measures about 6¼ (7½)" (16 [19] cm) from back of heel. To customize foot length, work even with MC until foot measures 1½ (1¾)" (3.8 [4.5] cm) less than desired finished length.

TOE

Rnd 1: On Needle 1, knit to last 3 sts, k2tog, k1; on Needle 2, k1, ssk, knit to last 3 sts, k2tog, k1; on Needle 3, k1, ssk, knit to end of needle—4 sts dec'd.

Rnd 2: Knit.

Rep Rnds 1 and 2 five (six) more times—24 (28) sts rem; 6 (7) sts each on Needle 1 and Needle 3, 12 (14) sts on Needle 2. Knit the sts from Needle 1 onto the end of Needle 3—12 (14) sts each on 2 needles.

FINISHING

With yarn threaded on a tapestry needle, use the Kitchener st (see Glossary, page 155) to graft sts tog. Weave in loose ends. Block lightly.

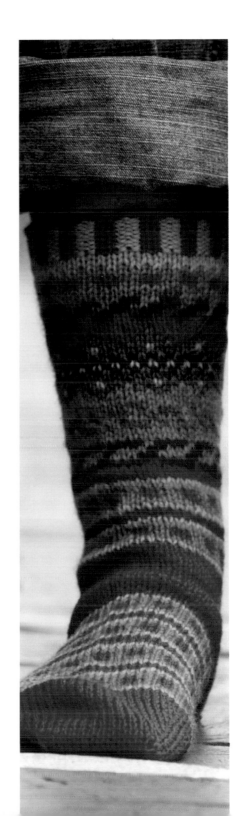

Kate Gilbert's thoroughly modern take on vintage paisley is captivating. She was inspired by the triangular shawls worn in nineteenth-century France and Spain that were worn wrapped around the body, crossed in the front, then tied in the back. Kate designed this one-color adaptation with those images in mind, but she brought this shawl beautifully into the twenty-first century by paring it down to a single color and using lacy restraint. She trimmed the shawl with an inconspicuous I-cord edging that doesn't distract from the paisley motifs.

STITCH GUIDE

3 Rows Unattached I-Cord: [K3, with RS still facing return 3 sts just worked to left needle] 2 times, k3—3 rows unattached I-cord completed.

K-yo-k Increase: Knit the first st on left needle but do not slip st from needle, yo, knit into the first st on left needle again, slip st from needle—2 sts inc'd; 3 sts made from 1 st.

P-yo-p Increase: Purl the first st on left needle but do not slip st from needle, yo, purl into the first st on left needle again, slip st from needle—2 sts inc'd; 3 sts made from 1 st.

I-Cord Edging with Double Increases (worked on 4 sts at each side):
RS rows: Work 3 rows unattached I-cord (see above) on first 3 sts, work k-yo-k inc (see above) in next st, work in pattern from chart to last 4 sts, k1, work 3 rows unattached I-cord on last 3 sts—2 sts inc'd inside I-cord edging at beg of RS rows.
WS rows: Sl 3 sts as if to purl with yarn in front (pwise wyf), work p-yo-p inc (see above) in next st, work in pattern from chart to last 4 sts, p1, sl 3 pwise wyf—2 sts inc'd inside I-cord edging at beg of WS rows.

FINISHED SIZE
About 86" (218.5 cm) across top edge and 28" (71 cm) from center of top edge to bottom point, after blocking.

YARN
Sportweight (#2 Fine).
Shown here: Garnstudio Silke Tweed (52% silk, 48% wool; 218 yd [200 m]/50 g): #14 pea green, 5 balls.

NEEDLES
Size 4 (3.5 mm): 40" (100 cm) or longer circular (cir). Adjust needle size if necessary to obtain the correct gauge.

NOTIONS
Smooth waste yarn in contrasting color for cast on; markers (m); tapestry needle.

GAUGE
About 24 stitches and 36 rows = 4" (10 cm) in stockinette stitch, before blocking; about 20 stitches and 32 rows = 4" (10 cm) in stockinette stitch, after blocking.

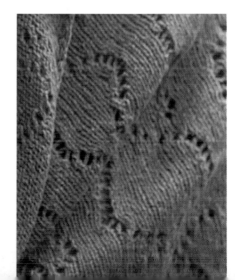

NOTES

❖ The scarf begins at the center of the top edge and worked down to the point. It is shaped by working double increases along the centerline and just inside the I-cord edgings at each side.

❖ Extra rows of unattached I-cord are worked at each end of RS rows to allow the top edge to stretch as needed during blocking.

❖ Charts 2, 3, 4, 5, and 6 each have been divided into two halves to fit the page. To establish the pattern for Row 1 of these divided charts, work the edging as established, then work the first half of the chart up to and including the center st, then work the second half of the chart, and finish by working the edging as established.

❖ To measure length while shawl is in progress, measure straight up from the center of the cast-on along a single column of stitches in the middle of either half of the shawl. Do not measure along the centerline because it is on the bias, and not on the true grain of the knitting (which is defined by a continuous single-stitch column).

❖ Join each new ball of yarn at the beginning or end of a row so the ends can be hidden inside the I-cord edging.

SHAWL

Using the provisional method (see Glossary, page 153), CO 3 sts. Work regular I-cord (see Glossary, page155) for 7 rows. *Next row:* With RS of I-cord still facing, pick up and knit 5 sts along side of I-cord, remove waste yarn from provisional cast-on, and place live sts released from base of cast-on edge on left needle—11 sts. Work 3 rows of unattached I-cord (see Stitch Guide) on the last 3 sts on needle (the sts from base of provisional cast-on), then turn work so WS is facing. *Next row:* (WS) Sl 3 as if to purl with yarn in front (pwise, wyf), p5, sl 3 pwise wyf. Working I-cord edging with double increases (see Stitch Guide) at each side, beg working in patt from Chart 1. The first 6 rows are written out in detail to get you started as foll:

Row 1: (RS) Work 3 rows unattached I-cord on first 3 sts, work k-yo-k inc (see Stitch Guide) in next st (counts as edging for beg of row), work Row 1 of chart over center 3 sts, work last 4 sts of row as k1, work 3 rows unattached I-cord on last 3 sts (counts as edging for end of row)—15 sts; 2 sts inc'd inside I-cord at beg of row, 2 sts inc'd at center as shown on chart.

Row 2: Sl 3 sts as if to purl with yarn in front (pwise wyf), work p-yo-p inc (see Stitch Guide) in next st (counts as edging for beg of row), work Row 2 of chart over next 7 sts, work last 4 sts as p1, sl 3 pwise wyf (counts as edging for end of row)—17 sts; 2 sts inc'd inside I-cord at beg of row.

Row 3: Work 3 rows of unattached I-cord on first 3 sts, work k-yo-k inc in next st (counts as edging at beg of row), work Row 3 of chart over next 9 sts, work last 4 sts of row as k1, work 3 rows of unattached I-cord on last 3 sts (counts as edging for end of row)—21 sts; 2 sts inc'd inside I-cord at beg of row, 2 sts inc'd at center according to chart.

Row 4: Sl 3 sts as if to purl with yarn in front, work p-yo-p inc in next st (counts as edging for beg of row), work Row 4 of chart over next 13 sts, work last 4 sts as p1, sl 3 pwise wyf (counts as edging for end of row)—23 sts; 2 sts inc'd I-cord at beg of row.

Row 5: Work 3 rows of unattached I-cord on first 3 sts, work k-yo-k inc in next st (counts as edging at beg of row), work Row 5 of chart over next 15 sts, work last 4 sts of row as k1, work 3 rows of unattached I-cord on last 3 sts (counts as edging for end of row)—27 sts; 2 sts inc'd inside I-cord at beg of row, 2 sts inc'd at center according to chart.

Row 6: Sl 3 sts as if to purl with yarn in front, work p-yo-p inc in next st (counts as edging for beg of row), work Row 6 of chart over next 19 sts, work last 4 sts as p1, sl 3 pwise wyf (counts as edging for end of row)—29 sts; 2 sts inc'd I-cord at beg of row.

Cont in this manner, working I-cord edging with double increases on the first 4 and last 4 sts of each row as established, until Row 22 of Chart 1 has been completed—77 sts; piece measures about 2¾" (7 cm) from beg (see Notes). The 2 sts inc'd inside the I-cord edging at the beg of the last WS row are not shown on the chart because they count as part of the edging until they are worked into the charted patt on the foll RS row. Change to Chart 2 (see Notes) and cont established edging sts at each side, work Rows 1–24 of chart—149 sts; piece measures about 5½" (14 cm) from beg. Change to Chart 3 and cont established edging at

With a little bit of imagination, a multicolored inspiration can become a single-colored creation.

each side, work Rows 1–28 of chart—233 sts; piece measures about 8½" (21.5 cm) from beg. Change to Chart 4 and cont established edging at each side, work Rows 1–32 of chart—329 sts; piece measures about 12" (30.5 cm) from beg. Change to Chart 5 and cont established edging at each side, work Rows 1–40 of chart—449 sts; piece measures about 16½" (42 cm) from beg. Change to Chart 6 and cont established edging at each side, work Rows 1–26 of chart—527 sts; piece measures about 19½" (49.5 cm) from beg. *Next row:* (RS) Work 3 rows of unattached I-cord on first 3 sts, work k-yo-k inc in next st, knit to center st, work k-yo-k inc in center st, knit to last 3 sts, BO next 2 sts—529 sts; last edging st will still be on needle after the BO gap. *Next row:* (WS) Working loosely, sl first st pwise wyf (the st before the gap), *k1 (2 sts on right needle), insert left needle into front of the 2 sts on right needle, k2tog tbl; rep from * until 3 sts rem, then BO rem 3 sts.

FINISHING

Weave in loose ends. Block to measurements.

Chart 1

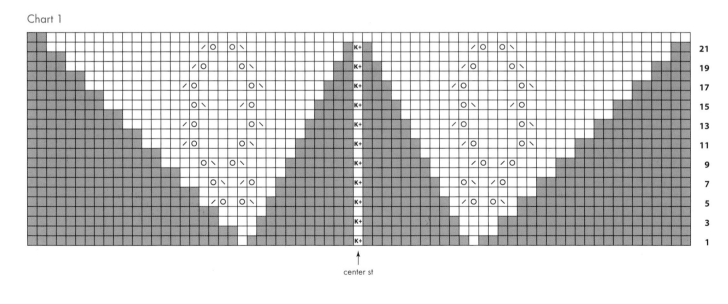

center st

| | k on RS; p on WS | | ╱ | k2tog | | K+ | k-yo-k inc (see Stitch Guide) | |
| | O | yo | | ╲ | ssk | | | no stitch | | pattern repeat |

Chart 2 First Half

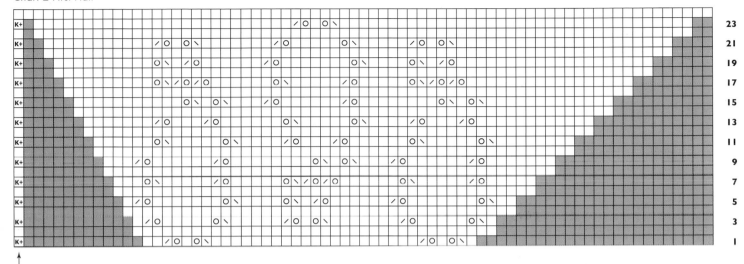

↑
center st

Chart 2 Second Half

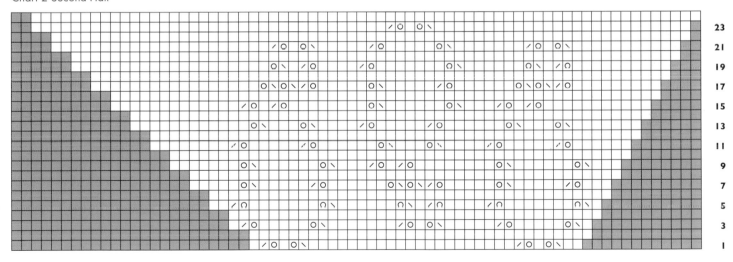

Chart 3 First Half

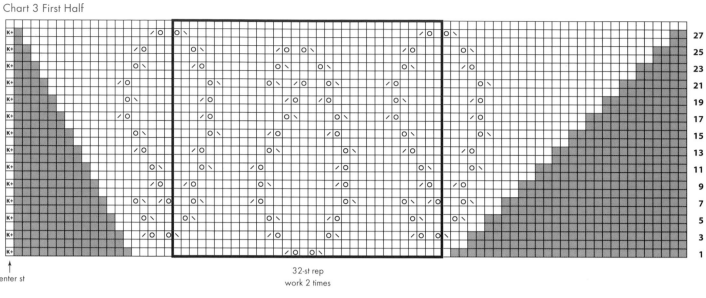

center st

32-st rep
work 2 times

Chart 3 Second Half

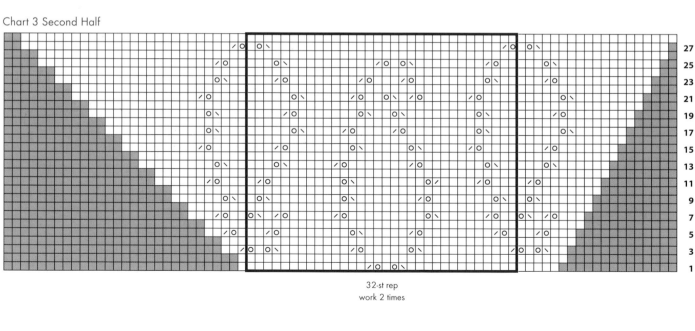

32-st rep
work 2 times

	k on RS; p on WS			/	k2tog		**K+**	k-yo-k inc (see Stitch Guide)
O	yo			\	ssk			no stitch
								pattern repeat

Chart 4 First Half

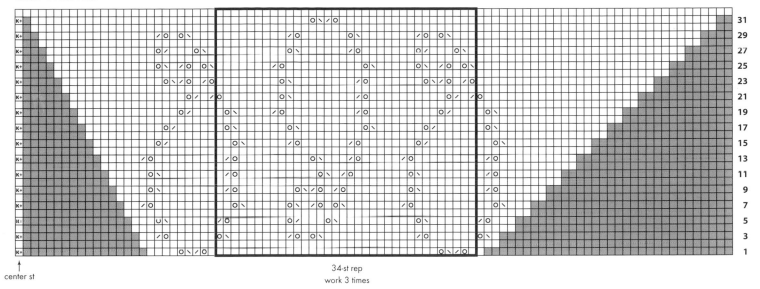

center st

34-st rep
work 3 times

Chart 4 Second Half

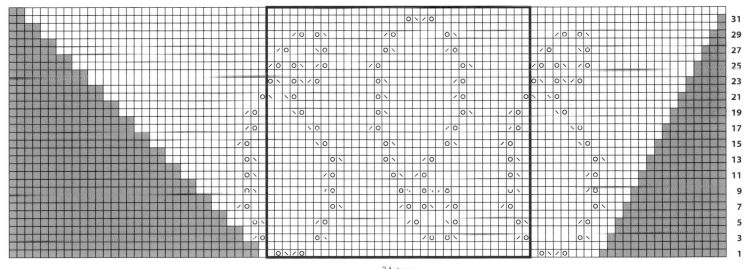

34-st rep
work 3 times

Chart 5 First Half

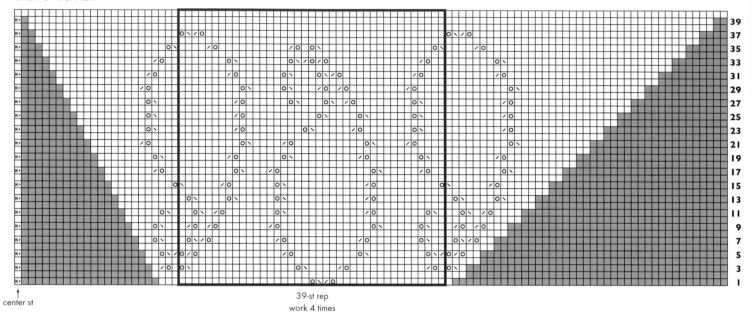

center st

39-st rep
work 4 times

Chart 5 Second Half

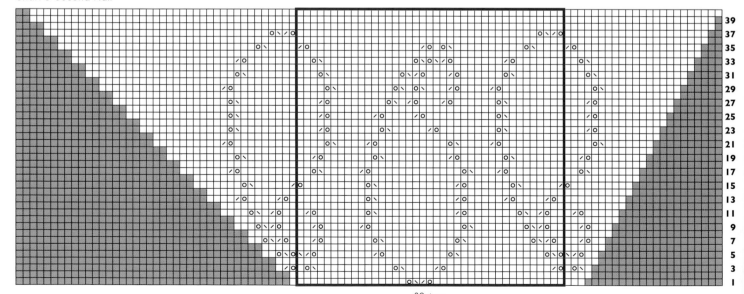

39-st rep
work 4 times

Chart 6 First Half

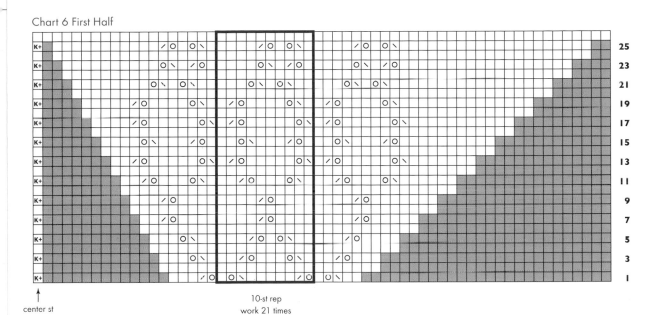

25
23
21
19
17
15
13
11
9
7
5
3
1

center st

10-st rep
work 21 times

Chart 6 Second Half

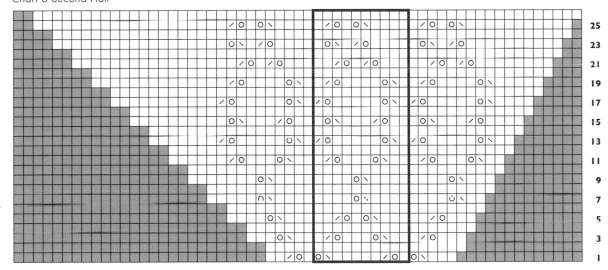

25
23
21
19
17
15
13
11
9
7
5
3
1

10-st rep
work 21 times

| | k on RS; p on WS | | / | k2tog | | K+ | k-yo-k inc (see Stitch Guide) |
| O | yo | | \ | ssk | | | no stitch | | | pattern repeat |

Try out new techniques
on small projects that
work up quickly.

piece measures about 8" (20.5 cm) from CO. *Next rnd:* Knit to first gusset m, remove m, place next 11 sts for gusset on holder or waste yarn, remove m, use the backward-loop method (see Glossary, page 152) to CO 1 st over gap, knit to end of rnd—35 sts.

Hand
Cont even until piece measures 2" (5 cm) from st CO at top of thumb gap. Change to tundra and knit 1 rnd. With tundra, BO all sts purlwise.

Thumb
Distribute 11 held gusset sts as evenly as possible on 3 dpn. With RS facing, join cocoa to end of thumb sts, then pick up and knit 1 st at base of CO for hand at top of thumb gap—12 sts total. Join for working in the rnd. Work even in St st until thumb measures 1" (2.5 cm) from joining rnd. Purl 1 rnd. Change to magenta and knit 1 rnd. With magenta, BO all sts purlwise.

FINISHING
Block to measurements.

Button Loops and Cuff Edging
Right mitt: With RS facing, join cocoa to left edge of cuff just above the magenta garter ridge. Using crochet hook, work button loops and crochet edging as foll: Work 1 crochet slip st (see Glossary, page 154, for crochet instructions) in selvedge of first St st row, *ch 3 for button loop, skip next 2 rows of knitting, work 1 slip st in each of next 3 rows of knitting; rep from * 4 more times, ch 3 for button loop, skip next 2 rows of knitting, work 1 slip st in each row of knitting to top of cuff slit, then work 1 slip st in each row of knitting to lower edge of cuff. Cut yarn and fasten off last st.
Left mitt: With RS facing, join cocoa to left edge of cuff just above the magenta garter ridge. Work 1 crochet slip st in each row of knitting to top of cuff slit. Examine right mitt and count the number of slip sts worked at the top of the slit above the last button loop, then work 1 slip st in each of the same number of rows of knitting, *ch 3 for button loop, skip next 2 rows of knitting, work 1 slip st in each of next 3 rows of knitting; rep from * 4 more times, ch 3 for button loop, skip next 2 rows of knitting, work 1 slip st in bottom row of knitting. Cut yarn and fasten off last st. With sewing needle and thread, sew 6 buttons to slit edge of each mitt, opposite buttonholes.

Needle Felting
Place needle felting mat inside hand warmer. Following template, at right, place a piece of magenta roving measuring about 1" by 1½" (2.5 by 3.8 cm) on back of glove for center of motif. Immerse kitchen sponge in hot, soapy water and squeeze a small amount on the magenta roving to dampen. With felting needle, gently poke section of roving repeatedly until roving has "felted" to the knitted fabric, adding roving as needed for desired coverage. Following template, add curlicue outline around center using plum roving. Add triangles on either side of main motif using

grey roving. Work a small circle above motif using tundra, then add random small dots of tundra to center of motif as shown. Work three chevron shapes below main motif using grey, tundra, and magenta as shown. Allow needle felting to air-dry thoroughly.

Embroidery

Work embroidery as shown on diagram using all six strands of embroidery floss (see pages 148–149, for embroidery stitches). Outline the inner and outer edges of main motif using grey floss and stem stitches. Work running stitches using plum floss just inside edges of grey triangles. Work random single stitches using plum floss in center of tundra circle above main motif. Work lines of running stitches in center of chevrons using plum floss on grey chevron, grey floss on tundra chevron, and green floss on magenta chevron.

Needle Felting and Embroidery Template

 tundra   plum
magenta   grey

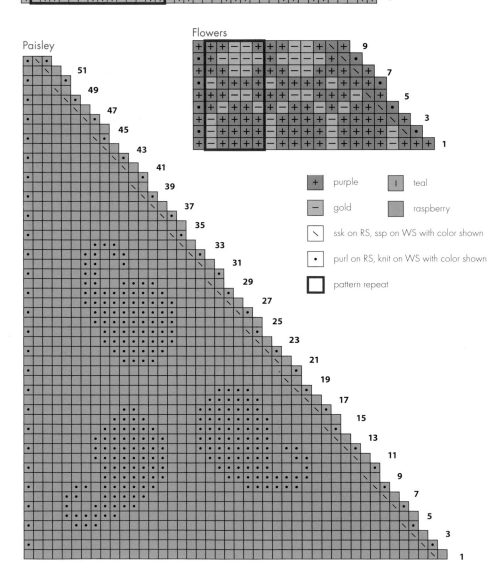

Diamonds

Paisley

Flowers

Legend:

+	purple	I	teal
−	gold		raspberry

\ ssk on RS, ssp on WS with color shown

· purl on RS, knit on WS with color shown

☐ pattern repeat

PILLOW FRONT

Triangle 1

With A, CO 73 sts.

Row 1: (RS) Knit.

Rows 2 and 4: (WS) K1, purl to last 3 sts, ssp (see Glossary, page 154), k1—1 st dec'd each row.

Rows 3 and 5: K1, ssk (see Glossary, page 154), knit to end—1 st dec'd each row; 69 sts rem after Row 5.

Row 6: K1, purl to last st, k1.

Rows 7 and 9: Rep Rows 3 and 5.

Rows 8 and 10: Rep Rows 2 and 4—65 sts rem after Row 10.

Rows 11–25: Work Rows 1–15 of Diamonds chart—53 sts rem.

Rows 26–30: Rep Rows 6–10—49 sts rem.

Rows 31–36: Rep Rows 1–6—45 sts rem after Row 35.

Rows 37–88: Change to B and work Rows 1–52 of Paisley chart—3 sts rem.

Row 89: With B, k1, ssk, pass first st over second to BO 1 st—1 st rem. Fasten off last st.

Triangle 2

Row 1: (RS) With C and RS facing, pick up and knit 73 sts evenly spaced along straight selvedge at left side of Triangle 1.

Rows 2–10: Work as for Triangle 1—65 sts rem after Row 10.

Rows 11–19: Work Rows 1–9 of Flowers chart—58 sts rem.

Row 20: Rep Row 2 of Triangle 1—57 sts rem.

Rows 21–25: Rep Rows 1–5 of Triangle 1—53 sts rem.

Rows 26–36: Work as for Triangle 1—45 sts rem after Row 35.

Rows 37–88: Change to B and work Rows 1–52 of Paisley chart—3 sts rem.

Row 89: Work as for Triangle 1.

Triangle 3

Row 1: (RS) With A and RS facing, pick up and knit 73 sts evenly spaced along straight selvedge at left side of Triangle 2.

Rows 2–89: Work as for Triangle 1.

Triangle 4

Row 1: (RS) With C and RS facing, pick up and knit 73 sts evenly spaced along straight selvedge at left side of Triangle 3.

Rows 2–89: Work as for Triangle 2.

FINISHING

With A threaded on a tapestry needle, sew the straight selvedge at left side of Triangle 4 to CO edge of Triangle 1. Lightly block pieces.

Embroidery

With C threaded on a tapestry needle, work herringbone st (see pages 148–149, for embroidery stitches), along color change line of Triangles 1 and 3 as shown in photograph. With A, work herringbone st along the color change line of Triangles 2 and 4. With D, work lines of coral knots along the CO edge of each triangle from outer edge to center, forming an X on the completed pillow front. With D, work a chain st outline around each purled paisley motif. With either A or C, work a second line of chain st just inside the chain st outline of each paisley motif.

Assembly

With RS of both back pieces facing, overlap garter st band of top flap over garter st band of bottom flap by about 1" (2.5 cm) and pin back pieces tog at sides. Place pinned back piece and front tog with WS touching and RS of both back and front facing out. With smooth, thin waste yarn threaded on tapestry needle, baste pieces tog around all 4 sides about ½" (1.3 cm) in from the edge. With RS facing and using A and crochet hook, work single crochet (sc; see Glossary, page 154) through both layers around all 4 sides to join pieces tog, working 4 sc in a single st at each corner. Remove basting yarn. Weave in loose ends. Sew buttons to bottom flap underneath buttonholes. Insert pillow form and use buttons to close.

What inspires you? A painting, a bowl, a textile? It may be as close as your cupboard or shelf.

Crown

Rnd 1: P1, *k2tog, p2; rep from * to last 3 sts, k2tog, p1—81 (87, 93) sts rem.

Rnd 2: P1, *k1, p2; rep from * to last 2 sts, k1, p1.

Rnds 3 and 4: Knit.

Rnds 5 and 6: Rep Rnd 2.

Rnds 7–10: Rep Rnds 3–6.

Rnd 11: *K2tog, k1; rep from * to end—54 (58, 62) sts rem.

Rnd 12: Knit.

Rnds 13 and 14: *K1, p1; rep from * to end.

Rnds 15 and 16: Knit

Rnd 17: *K2tog; rep from * to end of rnd—27 (29, 31) sts rem.

Rnds 18–20: Knit.

Rnd 21: *K2tog; rep from * to last st, k1—14 (15, 16) sts rem.

Rnd 22: Knit.

Rnd 23: [K2tog] 7 (7, 8) times, k0 (1, 0)—7 (8, 8) sts rem.

Cut yarn, leaving an 8" (20.5 cm) tail. Thread tail on a tapestry needle, draw through rem sts, pull tight to close hole at top of hat, and fasten off on WS. Weave in loose ends. Block lightly.

RIGHT MITTEN

CO 44 (48) sts. Place marker (pm) and join for working in the rnd, being careful not to twist sts.

Cuff

Next rnd: *K2, p2; rep from * to end. Rep the last rnd 23 more times—24 rnds total; piece measures about 2¼" (5.5 cm) from CO.

Lower Hand

Next rnd: *P1, M1 (see Glossary, page 155), p1, k20 (22); rep from * once more—46 (50) sts. *Next rnd:* *Work 3 sts in seed st border (see Stitch Guide), k20 (22); rep from * once more. *For larger size only,* rep the last rnd 2 more times—2 (4) rnds total completed above ribbed cuff. If not working optional initial, rep the last rnd 8 more times for both sizes, then skip to thumb gusset directions below—10 (12) rnds total completed above cuff; piece measures about 3¼ (3½)" (8.5 [9] cm) from CO. *Optional initial:* Establish position for your chosen letter from Alphabet chart (see page 122) on next rnd as foll: Work 3 sts in established seed st, k1 (2), work Rnd 1 of initial from Alphabet chart over next 2–12 sts depending on your chosen letter, knit to next seed st section, work 3 sts in established seed st, knit to end. Cont in patts for initial, St st, and seed st as established for 7 more rnds to complete initial—10 (12) rnds total completed above cuff—piece measures about 3¼ (3½)" (8.5 [9] cm) from CO.

Enjoy the powerful simplicity of knit-and-purl patterns.

Thumb Gusset

Next rnd: Work 3 sts in seed st, k20 (22), work 3 sts in seed st, pm, k3, M1, pm for end of thumb gusset, knit to end—4 sts between m for gusset. *Next rnd:* Work 1 rnd even in patt. *Next rnd:* Establish patt for back of hand and cont gusset shaping as foll: Work 3 sts in seed st, work Rnd 1 of Back of Hand chart over 20 (22) sts for back of hand as indicated for your size, work 3 sts in seed st, knit to end of gusset sts, M1, sl second gusset m, knit to end—1 st inc'd between gusset m. *Next rnd:* Work 1 rnd even in patt. Cont in patt, inc 1 st at end of gusset on the next rnd (Rnd 3 of chart), and then every other rnd 7 (9) more times, ending with Rnd 17 (21) of chart—13 (15) sts between gusset m; 56 (62) sts total. Work 3 rnds even in patt, ending with Rnd 20 (24) of chart—piece measures about 5½ (6)" (14 [15] cm) from CO. *Next rnd:* Work in patt to gusset sts, place 13 (15) gusset sts on holder, remove m at each end of gusset, use the backward-loop method (see Glossary, page 152) to CO 3 sts over gap, knit to end—46 (50) sts.

Upper Hand

Cont in patt until Rnd 40 of chart has been completed. Working sts for back of hand in St st, cont even until piece measures 7½ (8)" (19 [20.5] cm) from CO, or 1½ (1¾)" (3.8 [2] cm) less than desired total length.

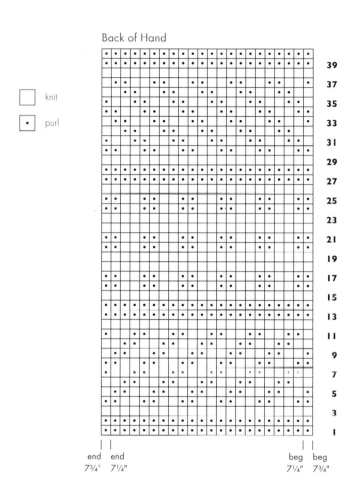

Back of Hand

knit

• purl

end 7¾" end 7¼"   beg 7¼" beg 7¾"

39 37 35 33 31 29 27 25 23 21 19 17 15 13 11 9 7 5 3 1

Shape Tip

Dec rnd: Work 3 st in seed st, ssk, knit to 2 sts before next seed st section, k2tog, work 3 sts in seed st, ssk, knit to last 2 sts, k2tog—4 sts dec'd. Work 1 rnd even in patt. Cont in patt, rep the shaping of the last 2 rnds 6 (7) more times, then work dec rnd once more—14 sts rem for both sizes. *Next rnd:* *Work 2 seed sts tog either as k2tog or p2tog to maintain patt, work 1 st in seed st, k4; rep from * once more—12 sts. Divide sts evenly on 2 needles (6 sts on each needle) for palm and back of hand. Cut yarn, leaving a 12" (30.5 cm) tail. Thread tail on a tapestry needle and use the Kitchener st (see Glossary, page 155) to graft sts tog, matching patts.

Alphabet

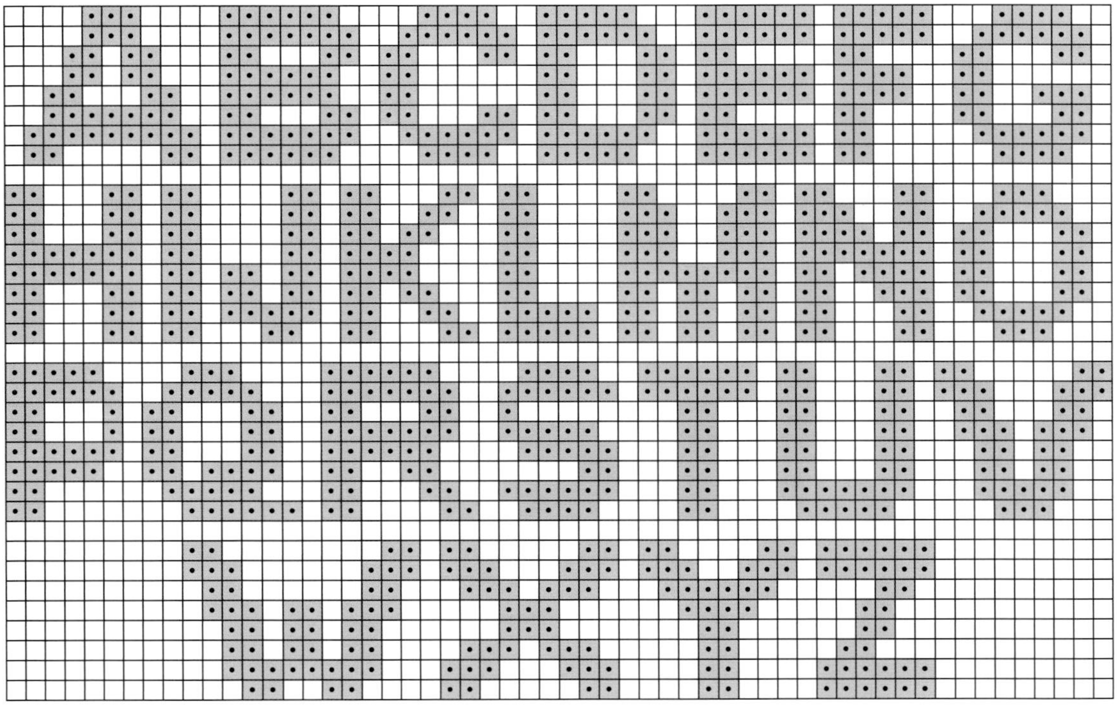

□ knit

• purl

Thumb

Return 13 (15) held gusset sts to needles with RS facing and rejoin yarn to end of thumb sts. Pick up and knit 3 sts along base of CO sts for hand at top of thumb gap, knit to end—16 (18) sts total. Join for working in the rnd and work even in St st until thumb measures 2 (2¼)" (5 [5.5 cm] or ½" (1.3 cm) less than desired length to tip of thumb. *Next rnd:* *K2tog; rep from *—8 (9) sts rem. *Next rnd:* [K2tog] 4 times, k0 (1)—4 (5) sts rem. Cut yarn, leaving an 8" (20.5 cm) tail. Thread tail on a tapestry needle, draw through rem sts, pull tight to close hole at tip of thumb, and fasten off on WS.

LEFT MITTEN

Cuff and Lower Hand

CO 44 (48) sts and work cuff and lower hand as for right mitten—46 (50) sts; piece measures about 3¼ (3½)" (8.5 [9] cm) from CO. *Note:* The placement of the initial on the left hand is deliberately not a mirror of the right-hand placement; on the right hand the initial is located below the little finger; on the left hand it is located next to the thumb.

Thumb Gusset

Next rnd: Work 3 sts in seed st, k20 (22), work 3 sts in seed st, k17 (21), pm for beg of thumb gusset, M1, k3—4 sts between m for gusset. *Next rnd:* Work 1 rnd even in patt. *Next rnd:* Establish patt for back of hand and cont gusset shaping as foll: Work 3 sts in seed st, work Rnd 1 of Back of Hand chart over 20 (22) sts for back of hand as indicated for your size, work 3 sts in seed st, knit to beg of gusset sts, sl gusset m, M1, knit to end—1 st inc'd between gusset m. *Next rnd:* Work 1 rnd even in patt. Cont in patt, inc 1 st at beg of gusset on the next rnd (Rnd 3 of chart), then every other rnd 7 (9) more times, ending with Rnd 17 (21) of chart 13 (15) sts between gusset m; 56 (62) sts total. Work 3 rnds even in patt, ending with Rnd 20 (24) of chart—piece measures about 5½ (6)" (14 [15] cm) from CO. *Next rnd:* Work in patt to gusset sts, remove m at beg of gusset, place 13 (15) gusset sts on holder, use the backward-loop method to CO 3 sts over gap—46 (50) sts.

Upper Hand, Shape Tip, and Thumb

Work as for right mitten.

FINISHING

Weave in loose ends. Block lightly.

SHIBORI-ESQUE NECK WRAP
MAGS KANDIS

Shibori is an age-old Japanese technique of folding, twisting, scrunching, stitching, and then dyeing fabric to achieve a color pattern. These days, we might call it tie-dye. To mimic the look of shibori—but without the laborious methods—**Mags Kandis** knitted a two-tone scarf, added contrasting crochet circles, then gathered the circles and felted the scarf to turn them into rounded puckers. To make the scarf stay put around the neck, Mags simply cut a slit in one end to accommodate the other end. The simple result makes a striking scarf.

SCARF

Before beginning to knit, wind off about 3 yd (3 meters) of A and set aside to use later for embroidery. With A, CO 42 sts. Work even in rev St st (purl RS rows; knit WS rows) until both balls of A have been used up (about 200 rows). Change to B and work even in rev St st until only about 48" (122 cm) of B is left (about 100 rows)—piece measures about 54" (137 cm) from CO, but exact length is not critical. BO all sts.

FINISHED SIZE
About 5¼" (13.5 cm) wide and 38" (96.5 cm) long. *Note:* Your exact finished size may be different because of individual variations in the felting process—that's part of the allure.

YARN
DK weight (#3 Light)).

Shown here: Classic Elite Miracle (50% alpaca; 50% Tencel; 108 yd [98 m]/50 g): #3332 gamay (burgundy; A) 2 balls; #3353 lady slipper (mauve; B) and #3350 pressed olive (olive; C), 1 ball each.

NEEDLES
Size 10 (6 mm). Adjust needle size if necessary to obtain the correct gauge.

NOTIONS
Tapestry needle; markers (m); dressmaker's water-soluble fabric marker (available at fabric stores) in contrasting color(s) to A and B; scissors; size J/10 (6 mm) crochet hook; mesh lingerie bag for felting.

GAUGE
14 stitches and 22 rows = 4" (10 cm) in reverse stockinette stitch (rev St st), before felting.

FINISHING

Weave in loose ends.

Crochet Rings (make 8)

With C and crochet hook, ch 30 (see Glossary, page 154 for crochet instructions). Join with a slip st to form ring. Cut yarn, leaving a 12" (30.5 cm) tail. Make 7 more crochet rings in the same manner. On RS of scarf, count up 80 rows from CO edge at the A end of the scarf and draw a line across the scarf with water-soluble fabric marker to mark embroidery area. Using tails, sew crocheted rings randomly to RS of scarf between CO edge and marker line as shown in photograph. With A threaded on a tapestry needle, sew a line of basting sts around the open center of each crochet ring as close as possible to inside edge of the ring. With RS still facing, draw up ends of basting thread tightly to form a "bubble" of fabric in the center of each ring. Tie ends of basting thread securely so bubbles will maintain their shape throughout the felting process.

Experiment with non-knit techniques to expand your design repertoire.

Felting

Place scarf in lingerie bag. Add a small amount of mild detergent and run through normal washing-machine cycle set for a small load and hot water, stopping the washer periodically to check felting progress. *Note:* It may take more than one cycle to achieve the desired amount of felting. When piece is sufficiently felted and the individual stitches are no longer visible, remove scarf from washer, pull into shape, and allow to dry flat.

Slit

Using water-soluble fabric marker, draw a line to indicate the position of a 3½" (9 cm) slit centered on the B end of the scarf, beg about 4½" (11.5 cm) down from BO edge. Carefully cut slit open along marked line. The felted fabric will not ravel and the edges of the slit will need no additional reinforcement,

BOGOLANFINI PULLOVER
FIONA ELLIS

Fiona Ellis took the color palette and patterning inspired by African textiles and crossed them with the traditional Northern European knitting technique of Fair Isle or stranded knitting. The colored patterns used on the body alternate between very traditional Fair Isle motifs and those derived from African mud-resist printed cloths. The textured repeat used for the sleeves and yoke directly mirrors graphic African patterns. The African influence is further referenced in the choice of zebra-like patterned buttons at the keyhole neckline.

STITCH GUIDE

Textured Pattern (multiple of 6 sts + 1):
Rows 1, 5, and 7: (RS) K2, *p2, k4; rep from * to last 5 sts, p2, k3.
Rows 2 and 4: *P4, k2; rep from * to last st, p1.
Row 3: *P2, k4; rep from * to last st, p1.
Row 6: Purl.
Row 8: P2, *k2, p4; rep from * to last 5 sts, k2, p3.
Row 9: *K4, p2; rep from * to last st, k1.
Row 10: P2, *k2, p4; rep from * to last 5 sts, k2, p3.
Row 11: K2, *p2, k4; rep from * to last 5 sts, p2, k3.
Row 12: Purl.
Repeat Rows 1–12 for pattern.

Armhole and Sleeve Cap Decreases:
RS rows: K1, ssk (see Glossary, page 154), work in patt to last 3 sts, k2tog, k1—2 sts dec'd.
WS rows: P1, p2tog, work in patt to last 3 sts, ssp (see Glossary, page 154), p1—2 sts dec'd.

> **NOTE**
> ❖ In Chart C, Rows 6 and 8 are deliberately not the same. There are extra purple sts in Row 6 that do not appear in Row 8, so the main purple motif resembles a letter M.

FINISHED SIZE
35½ (39, 42½, 46½, 50)" (90 [99, 108, 118, 127] cm) bust/chest circumference. Sweater shown measures 39" (99 cm).

YARN
DK weight (#3 Light).
Shown here: Blue Sky Alpacas Alpaca-Silk (50% alpaca, 50% silk; 146 yd [133 m]/ 50 g): #130 mandarin (orange; MC), 7 (8, 9, 9, 10) skeins; #134 iron (charcoal) and #110 ecru, 2 (2, 2, 3, 3) skeins each; #131 kiwi (light green), #137 sapphire (light blue), and #129 amethyst (purple), 1 skein each.

NEEDLES
Body—sizes 6, 5, and 4 (4, 3.75, and 3.5 mm): straight. Neckband—size 5 (3.75 mm): 16" (40 cm) circular (cir). Adjust needle size if necessary to obtain the correct gauge.

NOTIONS
Stitch holders; tapestry needle; two ⅞" (2.2 cm) buttons.

GAUGE
26 stitches and 26 Rows = 4" (10 cm) in stockinette-stitch color-work patterns from charts on largest needles; 24 stitches and 32 rows = 4" (10 cm) in textured pattern on smallest needles, 20 stitches and 29 rows = 4" (10 cm) in textured pattern on middle-size needles.

BACK

With charcoal and middle-size needles, CO 110 (122, 134, 146, 158) sts. Beg with a RS row, knit 4 rows, inc 5 sts evenly spaced in last WS row—115 (127, 139, 151, 163) sts; piece measures about ½" (1.3 cm) from CO. Change to largest needles.

Rows 1–15: Work Rows 1–15 of Chart A.

Rows 16–18: With charcoal, purl 3 rows, beg and ending with a WS row.

Rows 19–23: Work Rows 1–5 of Chart B.

Rows 24–26: With charcoal, purl 3 rows.

Rows 27–39: Work Rows 1–13 of Chart C (see Note).

Rows 40–42: With charcoal, purl 3 rows.

Rows 43–47: Work Rows 1–5 of Chart D.

Rows 48–50: With charcoal, purl 3 rows.

Rows 51–63: Work Rows 1–13 of Chart E.

Rows 64–74: Rep Rows 16–26.

Rows 75–89: Work Rows 1–15 of Chart A.

Rows 90–97: Rep Rows 40–47.

Rows 98 and 99: With charcoal, purl 2 rows, ending with a RS row.

Row 100: (WS) Change to MC and smallest needles, and purl 1 row—piece measures about 15" (38 cm) from CO.

4¼ (5, 6, 6¾, 7¾)"
11 (12.5, 15, 17, 19.5) cm

6¾ (7¼, 7¼, 7½, 7¾)"
17 (18.5, 18.5, 19, 19.5) cm

¾"
2 cm

7¼ (7½, 7¾, 8½, 8½)"
18.5 (19, 19.5, 21.5, 21.5) cm

2¼ (2½, 2½, 3, 3)"
5.5 (6.5, 6.5, 7.5, 7.5) cm

3"
7.5 cm

Front & Back

15 (15, 15½, 16, 16½)"
38 (38, 39.5, 40.5, 42) cm

17¾ (19½, 21¼, 23¼, 25)"
45 (49.5, 54, 59, 63.5) cm

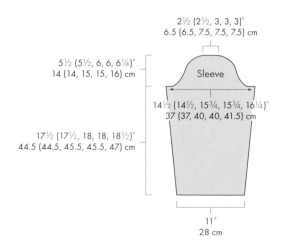

2½ (2½, 3, 3, 3)"
6.5 (6.5, 7.5, 7.5, 7.5) cm

Sleeve

5½ (5½, 6, 6, 6¼)"
14 (14, 15, 15, 16) cm

14½ (14½, 15¾, 15¾, 16¼)"
37 (37, 40, 40, 41.5) cm

17½ (17½, 18, 18, 18½)"
44.5 (44.5, 45.5, 45.5, 47) cm

11"
28 cm

Chart A

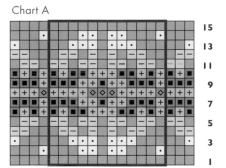

15
13
11
9
7
5
3
1

Chart B

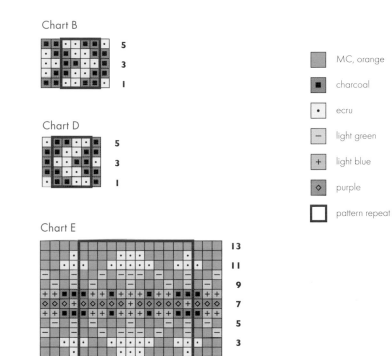

5
3
1

Chart D

5
3
1

Chart C

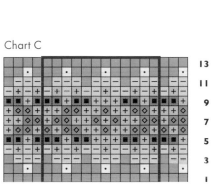

13
11
9
7
5
3
1

Chart E

13
11
9
7
5
3
1

◻ (gray)	MC, orange
◼	charcoal
•	ecru
−	light green
+	light blue
◇	purple
▢	pattern repeat

Sizes 35½ (39)" only: Skip to Shape Armholes below, and work in textured patt (see Stitch Guide).

Sizes 42½ (46½, 50)" only: Work even in textured patt (see Stitch Guide) until piece measures 15½ (16, 16½)" (39.5 [40.5, 42] cm) from CO, ending with a WS row.

Shape Armholes

Cont in textured patt, BO 4 sts at beg of next 2 rows—107 (119, 131, 143, 155) sts rem. Beg with next RS row, dec 1 st each end of needle (see Stitch Guide) on the next 7 rows, work 1 WS row even, then dec 1 st each end of needle on foll RS row—91 (103, 115, 127, 139) sts. Cont even in textured patt until armholes measure 7¼ (7½, 7¾, 8½, 8½)" (18.5 [19, 19.5, 21.5, 21.5] cm), ending with a WS row.

Shape Shoulders

With RS facing and cont in patt, BO 8 (10, 12, 14, 15) sts at beg of next 4 rows, then BO 9 (10, 12, 13, 16) sts at beg of foll 2 rows—41 (43, 43, 45, 47) sts rem. Place sts on holder for back neck.

FRONT

CO 110 (122, 134, 146, 158) sts and work as for back until armholes measure 2 (2, 2¼, 2½, 2½)" (5 [5, 5.5, 6.5, 6.5] cm), ending with a WS row—91 (103, 115, 127, 139) sts rem.

Shape Neck

With RS facing and cont in patt, work 44 (50, 56, 62, 68) sts, k2tog at center front, join new ball of yarn, work in patt to end—45 (51, 57, 63, 69) sts at each side. Working each side separately and keeping 3 sts on each side of front neck slit in garter st (knit every row), cont in patt until piece measures 3" (7.5 cm) from dividing row, ending with a WS row.

Shape Left Front Neck and Shoulder

With RS facing, work 40 (46, 52, 58, 64) left front sts in patt, place last 5 sts of left front on holder. Place 45 (51, 57, 63, 69) sts for right front on a separate holder to work later. Cont in patt on left front sts, BO 6 sts at beg of next WS row, then dec 1 st at neck edge every row 9 (10, 10, 11, 12) times—25 (30, 36, 41, 46) sts rem. Cont even in patt until armhole measures 7¼ (7½, 7¾, 8½, 8½)" (18.5 [19, 19.5, 21.5, 21.5] cm), ending with a WS row. Cont in patt, at armhole edge (beg of RS rows), BO 8 (10, 12, 14, 15) sts 2 times, then BO rem 9 (10, 12, 13, 16) sts.

Shape Right Front Neck and Shoulder

Return 45 (51, 57, 63, 69) sts for right front to needle with RS facing. Place first 5 sts of right front on holder—40 (46, 52, 58, 64) sts rem. Rejoin MC to beg of sts on needle with RS facing. BO 6 sts at beg of first RS row, then dec 1 st at neck edge every row 9 (10, 10, 11, 12) times—25 (30, 36, 41, 46) sts rem. Cont even in patt until armhole measures 7¼ (7½, 7¾, 8½, 8½)" (18.5 [19, 19.5, 21.5, 21.5] cm), ending with a RS row. Cont in patt, at armhole edge (beg of WS rows), BO 8 (10, 12, 14, 15) sts 2 times, then BO rem 9 (10, 12, 13, 16) sts.

SLEEVES

With MC and middle-size needles, CO 50 sts. Beg with a RS row, knit 4 rows, inc 5 sts evenly spaced in last WS row—55 sts; piece measures about ½" (1.3 cm) from CO. Beg with RS Row 1, work textured patt for 10 (10, 6, 6, 6) rows. *Inc row:* (RS) K1, M1 (see Glossary, page 155), work in patt to last st, M1, k1—2 sts inc'd. Work inc row every 14 (14, 12, 12, 10)th row 5 (5, 1, 1, 10) more time(s), then work inc row every 12 (12, 10, 10, 8)th row 3 (3, 10, 10, 2) times, working new sts into patt—73 (73, 79, 79, 81) sts. Cont even in patt until piece measures 17½ (17½, 18, 18, 18½)" (44.5 [44.5, 45.5, 45.5, 47] cm) from CO, ending with a WS row.

Shape Cap

Cont in patt, BO 4 sts at beg of next 4 rows—57 (57, 63, 63, 65) sts rem. Dec 1 st each end of needle (see Stitch Guide) every RS row 16 (16, 18, 18, 19) times—25 (25, 27, 27, 27) sts

Remember to account for different gauges when mixing patterns and textures.

rem. BO 3 sts at beg of next 4 rows—13
(13, 15, 15, 15) sts rem. BO all sts.

FINISHING

Weave in loose ends. Block pieces to
measurements. With yarn threaded on
a tapestry needle, sew front to back at
shoulders.

Neckband

With MC, cir needle, RS facing, and beg
at right front neck, k5 held sts, pick up
and knit 22 (22, 24, 26, 28) sts evenly
spaced along right front neck, k41 (43,
43, 45, 47) held back neck sts, pick up
and knit 22 (22, 24, 26, 28) sts evenly
spaced along left front neck, k5 held
sts—95 (97, 101, 107, 113) sts total. Knit
5 rows. Loosely BO all sts.

With yarn threaded on a tapestry needle,
sew sleeve caps into armholes. Sew
sleeve and side seams. Sew a button to
top corner on each side of front neck slit.
With yarn threaded on a tapestry needle,
anchor yarn to top of right front slit opposite left button, make a yarn loop big
enough to fit over button, then anchor the
end of the loop in the same place where
you began. Work closely spaced buttonhole stitches (see page 148) all the way
around the strand of the button loop to
reinforce it. Block lightly again if desired.

designNOTEBOOK

The projects in *Folk Style* demonstrate many ways that global influences can be incorporated into fresh, contemporary designs. At least some of the elements in each design are based on traditional motifs, silhouettes, and/or techniques, which are not necessarily associated with knitting. The *Folk Style* designers took inspiration from baskets, quilts, weavings, tapestries, and printed textiles, as well as traditional knitwear. They translated their ideas into knitted stitches and surface embellishments, including embroidery, appliqué, and felting, to highlight and emphasize the folk roots of their designs. And you can do it, too. Simply follow the guidelines provided here and in no time you'll be creating your own folk-inspired design.

FINDING INSPIRATION

Today's knitters have a vast array of materials to draw upon for inspiration—centuries of design ideas from diverse cultures that display a wealth of color, texture, and motif possibilities. It was not that long ago that information on and images of ethnic or folk art, craft, and textiles could be accessed only through research libraries or museums. But now, books, magazines, television, movies, and the Internet provide easy access to a host of resources for inspiration (and techniques). Check out the Bibliography on page 159 for a list of books, publications, and websites that I find particularly useful.

The cornerstone of any successful design is an inspired idea. The sources for inspiration are endless. Perhaps it's the particular color or texture of a skein of yarn; perhaps it's a process, such as felting or embroidery; perhaps an object, such as a shard of Incan pottery, a medieval tapestry, or a piece of Italian jewelry. It doesn't matter what jumpstarts your creativity—it only matters that you jump on board with it.

For decades, knitting designers have taken inspiration from woven and printed textiles, new and old. Japanese kimonos, American patchwork quilts, and Middle Eastern kilim rugs are examples of beautiful multicolored textiles that are based on small repeating shapes or motifs. It's easy to translate these patterns into knitted cloth. All you need is some graph paper, a few colored pencils, and time to play.

Don't be afraid to depart from your initial plans at any time as you design and create on your own. Keep in mind that your design doesn't need to be—and indeed, shouldn't be—an exact representation of the object of your inspiration. Feel free to mix traditions. Add a bit of North American folk art to a Peruvian cap; stir some African flavor into a Fair Isle pullover; mix a little Old World spice into a modern silhouette. In designing, a bit of disobedience is encouraged—merge, meld, and morph your ideas!

SILHOUETTE

A good place to find inspiration is in the silhouette or shape of a folk garment or object. History and cultures are bursting with highly recognizable silhouettes—Ming-dynasty vases, South American earflap hats, Japanese kimonos. By simply duplicating these shapes, you can add a distinctive folk element to your own design. Annie Modesitt borrowed the asymmetrical closure and stand-up collar typical of Chinese garments in Shanghai Surplice (page 72) and Kristin Nicholas created a modern rendition of a traditional Moroccan hat in her Sunny Flower Fez (page 68).

Look to knitting books and magazines for silhouette inspirations. Schematics (the line drawings of garment shapes that accompany written instructions) clearly show the shape of each piece of a garment, along with valuable measurements to guide you in your own designs. For more ideas, check out books of traditional folk costume at the library.

COLOR

Color is an important part of every design, especially those with roots in folk tradition. Pay attention to your surroundings and you'll find inspiring color combinations everywhere: a charcoal gray house with deep red trim; a bed of gold and lilac flowers bordering a milky white garden shed; a red-haired girl in a soft blue dress; the saturated blue of indigo softened by paler patterning. It's a good idea to always have a notebook—or at least a paper napkin—handy to jot down colors and color combinations that catch your attention. Make note of whatever speaks to you. When you're home, dig through your yarn stash and steal snippets of yarn or color chips of the colors as you remember them and tape them into an "idea book." Review your idea book from time to time—you never know when one of the color combinations will spark an idea.

Mother Nature is the ultimate colorist. She never goes wrong when seeding a field with wild-flowers, setting a sun behind mountains, or changing leaves in anticipation of winter. You'll always succeed if you take your cue from nature. Gayle Bunn mimicked the colors in a painting of an autumn landscape in her Algonquin Socks (page 90). Tara Jon Manning created her own spring palette of soft lilac and cornflower blue against a sandy background in her Annie Oakley Jacket (page 56).

Many designers turn to textiles for color inspiration. The original designer of the textile already worked out a pleasing palette—possibly years (or centuries) ago and miles away, but that's okay! Marilyn Webster turned to her sari collection when deciding on the rich colors in her Indian Silk Pillow (page 114). Another good source of color inspiration is as close as the paint department at your neighborhood home-improvement center. Paint colors look as good knitted into a project as painted on a wall.

SHANGHAI SURPLICE
annie modesitt

ALGONQUIN SOCKS
gayle bunn

- Patterns or motifs to use as inspiration

- Plain white cardstock, about 6" (15 cm) square (the thin cardboard that is often included with nylon stocking or tights packaging works well)

- Pencil and/or marker

- Ruler

- Scissors

WINDOW BOX EXERCISE

Try this design exercise to train your eye to isolate motifs (from any source) that can be translated into your own designs.

STEP 1

Gather a few pages of inspiration that you don't mind cutting up (or make photocopies): magazines, postcards, photographs, wrapping paper, wallpaper, etc.

STEP 2

Use a pencil or marker and ruler to draw two 6" (15 cm) L-shaped cropping tools on the cardstock. Cut out the shapes.

Place the cropping tools on top of your inspiration source. Expand, contract, lengthen, and widen them to create different "windows" of ideas. Move them around until you find an area that inspires you.

STEP 3

Cut out the image and save it with other inspiration ideas. Take it a step further by cutting out a silhouette of a garment and moving it around your images to see how the pattern might translate into a garment.

STEP 4

Swatch the pattern to see how you like it as knitted fabric.

If you're like me, you'll find this is much more "fun" than "exercise"!

EXPERIMENTATION

You can spend hours reading about and studying color theory. While this will give you a cerebral understanding, you won't really learn it until you put it into practice. When you find a color combination you like, don't be tempted to assume it will look as good when knitted into stitches. Colors that look great side by side may look quite different when knitted up next to each other. For example, a yarn that appears gray may surprisingly turn to a mossy green when worked close to purple, if that gray has a green undertone. A gray with a blue undertone will appear bluish when worked close to yellow. Stark white may appear "fresh" in the ball, but may be *too* white when worked with dark colors—natural or cream might be a better choice. Sometimes just a little bit of particular color can add a lively touch, but more than that may border on repulsive. Even professional designers swatch their color ideas before they begin full-scale projects. You'll be amazed how colors change when knitted together side by side in stripes or in a Fair Isle pattern—they can look completely different depending on what other colors are nearby.

If you're just starting to work with color, try Gayle Bunn's Algonquin Socks (page 96). Make them just as she did or choose eight colors of your own. Use the colors in one arrangement on the first sock, then shake them up for the mate. You'll learn a lot about color interactions and end up with a lively pair of mismatched, but coordinating, socks that are as much fun to wear as they were to knit.

The more confident you become working with color, the more adventurous you'll feel. Try using unconventional color combinations for motifs with strong traditional roots. For example, in its traditional application, the Nordic star motif in Ann Budd's Nordic Star (page 86) is knitted in natural against navy or red. But by choosing two hot shades of rich burgundy and burnt orange, Ann gave the motif a whole new look.

Experiment: Something you think will work may not. And something you think will not work just might.

Colors look different depending on what other colors are nearby.

ANNIE OAKLEY JACKET

tara jon manning

INDIAN SILK PILLOW

marilyn webster

YARNS

What kind of yarn do you choose—flat, shiny, thick, thin, smooth, nubby? Wool, cotton, linen, silk, bamboo, even corn! Ultimately, yarn choice in a personal decision that you'll base on many variables, including fiber content, color, gauge, drape, care, and cost.

Just as you'll never really know how colors work until you knit them up together, you can't be sure if a yarn is right for your design until you knit with it. Because this can involve time and expense, take advantage of all the help you can get. Yarn shops are virtual encyclopedias of yarn information—balls and balls of yarn to examine, knowledgeable staff to answer questions, sample garments and/or swatches that show how the yarns knit up, and shelves of books, magazines, and patterns that suggest particular yarns for particular projects. Click on the Internet to find websites that offer everything from personal blogs by knitters to full-fledged yarn reviews. Even if you don't have a particular ball of yarn in your possession, you can learn a lot about its personality and suitability for your design by reading about it on the Internet.

To create a frontier "feel" of buckskin in her Annie Oakley Jacket (page 56), Tara Jon Manning chose a softly textured yarn and worked it in simple stockinette stitch (which, by the way, made the perfect backdrop for delicate embroidery). The bright silk yarn Marilyn Webster used in her Indian Silk Pillow (page 114) radiates the lush and exotic allure of Indian textiles. As nice as it is to side with convention; it's also a good idea to shake things up from time to time. By choosing "unexpected" yarns, you can give your design a pleasing sense of contradiction. For my Modern Quilt Wrap (page 24), I took inspiration from the sturdy patchwork quilts of the nineteenth century, but worked it in a weightless mohair-silk yarn. The utilitarian basket that inspired Gina Wilde's Appalachian Gathering Basket (page 62) would never be woven in silk, but a wool-silk blend is the perfect choice for her knitted version.

GETTING IDEAS OUT OF YOUR HEAD AND ONTO PAPER

Okay, so your brain is full of ideas for motifs, pattern stitches, silhouette, color, and yarn . . . now what? You can sit back and let these ideas percolate in your mind until they brew up the perfect combination or you can take a more proactive (and more reliable) approach. To turn those ideas into a successful project, you'll want to gather some paper, colored pencils, yarn, and needles.

Begin by sketching your ideas on paper. Draw a silhouette and sketch in your motif(s) to see where they look best. Use colored pencils to represent your color choices. Don't worry if you lack drawing skills—simply trace or photocopy designs from other sources (use a light table or place your work against a bright window to facilitate tracing). Play around with the size and proportion. Use a photocopier or scanner to blow it up, shrink it down, center it, skew it, then start all over again. Use your colored pencils to make the patterns quiet and subdued, then lively and bright. Don't be surprised if you find that your initial idea is not the one you like best.

In her Nordic Star (page 86), Ann Budd isolated a traditional six-point Scandinavian star motif, blew it up to giant proportion, and positioned it smack in the center of a cropped sweater. To add to the modern flavor, she chose nontraditional colors. Gayle Bunn took a similar approach in her Felt Appliquéd Skirt (page 90) and worked large-scale appliqué and embroidery as a playful translation of fine crewelwork.

Once you have a motif or pattern in mind, plot it on graph paper, allowing each square to represent one stitch. For color patterns, simply fill in the squares with the appropriate colors. For stitch patterns, use symbols (leave the square blank for knit stitches; use a dot for purl stitches, etc.). If possible, use proportional knitter's graph paper, which takes into account the rectangular shape of knitted stitches (look closely—each stitch is wider than it is tall). Grab some yarn and needles and knit a swatch of your design. If you don't like what you see, make adjustments and knit another swatch. Keep going until you find the look you want.

Unless you're already comfortable designing projects from scratch, use a pattern that already exists as a template for your folk-inspired design. As long as your gauge matches, you can substitute or add your own pattern, motif, or color-work design without having to change stitch counts. Otherwise, turn to the Bibliography (page 159) for some of the books that provide in-depth explanations on how to create shapes and determine fit. If you use a computer, look for knitting software that helps you create shapes and charts with a click of your mouse.

NORDIC STAR
ann budd

TECHNIQUES

Now that you have a design worked out, it's a simple matter of using conventional knitting techniques to turn your idea into reality. Most folk traditions celebrate colors, textures, and embellishments.

WORKING WITH COLOR

One thing you will quickly notice about the projects in *Folk Style* is the abundance of color. In fact, only two of the designs included are worked in single colors. Basically, there are two ways of working with color: knitting it right into the stitches (stripes, Fair Isle, or intarsia) and adding it on with stitching and/or embellishments. Don't feel you have to limit yourself to only one method of working with color—combine techniques for even more visual excitement.

Stripes

The simplest way to add color is to knit stripes. Stripes involve working with just one color at a time and all of the stitches in a row are worked in the same color. Ann Budd's Burma Rings Scarf (page 46) is based on stripes of several colors of similar hues. She worked the scarf side to side to orient the stripes lengthwise. Although it's not apparent, I also knitted stripes in my Modern Quilt Wrap (page 24), but because I worked a mitered-square pattern at the same time, the result is anything but stripy.

Fair Isle Method

In Fair Isle knitting (also called color stranding), two (or more) colors are worked across a row according to a charted pattern; the color not in use is carried loosely across the back of the work. Both colors extend across the entire row, making a fabric of double thickness—one yarn forms a strand across the back while the other forms the stitches. Fair Isle knitting can be worked circularly in rounds or back and forth in rows. Much of the color work in Gayle Bunn's Algonquin Socks (page 96) and Fiona Ellis's Bogolanfini Pullover (page 128) is worked in the Fair Isle technique with no more than two colors per row. But by changing the colors, these designers added punch to their designs.

Intarsia Method

With intarsia knitting, the colors are isolated in discrete areas, called color blocks, and each area is worked with a separate ball of yarn. The blocks can have vertical, horizontal, diagonal, or curved boundaries, which makes intarsia ideal for organic, fluid color designs. Just about anything you can draw on paper can be reproduced with intarsia. Because there is no stranding, the fabric is less likely to pucker and less bulky than its Fair Isle counterpart. Intarsia designs are most easily knitted back and forth in rows, although there are techniques for working it in rounds. Depending on the size of your project and the number of colors, there can be dozens of balls of yarn hanging off the needles. Check out the tips below for ways to manage them.

Di Gilpin used intarsia to work the organic looking design in her Grand Tour Waistcoat (page 38). For more visual interest, she added a textured stitch pattern in the background color. Lisa B. Evans went geometric in her colorful Tribal Baby Carrier (page 80) by working small square blocks of color in a radiating pattern to create colorful diamonds. She also added stripes and textured stitches for a riotous play of color.

Don't feel the need to limit yourself to one type of color work. Many folk traditions are based on bold color expressions that are best translated into knitting through a variety of techniques. Gayle Bunn went wild with her Patchwork Jacket (page 18) and worked her intarsia blocks in Fair Isle patterns.

Whatever type of color work you choose, chances are that you'll have a lot of loose ends to work in before you're done. Although you can follow the color boundaries as you weave in the ends, the wrong side of the work is inherently messier than the right. If this bothers you, consider adding a lining. The one that Lisa B. Evans added to her Tribal Baby Carrier gives a tidy interior and adds welcome strength and support to the piece.

PATCHWORK JACKET
gayle bunn

TIPS FOR INTARSIA KNITTING

❖ Before you begin an intarsia pattern, familiarize yourself with the chart. Identify the areas that require separate "balls" of yarn and prepare these balls in advance.

❖ Instead of working with full balls of yarn, measure out lengths of yarn in 2 to 3 foot (61 to 91.5 cm) lengths for small blocks of color (the loose ends are much easier to pull out of tangles than bobbins). For larger areas, wind the yarn into mini pull-skeins or yarn butterflies as shown below.

❖ Take a few minutes to estimate how much yarn you'll need for each color block before you cut the yarn. For small areas of color, it's easy. A 2 to 3 foot (61 to 91.5 cm) length of yarn is usually all you'll need. For larger areas, do a rough count of the stitches (you don't need to be exact). Let's say that you need to work an area of 110 stitches and let's say that you're working with worsted-weight yarn at a gauge of 5 stitches to the inch. Divide the number of stitches by the gauge to get a very rough estimate of the surface area involved (for our example we'll divide 110 by 5 to get 22"). Then (this is the magic part), multiply this number by 3 to estimate the length of yarn, in inches, needed to work stockinette stitch. In our example, we'll need a "ball" of yarn about 66" (167.5 cm) long. For safety, add 12" (30.5 cm) or so to allow for tails to be woven in later.

❖ After working in the yarn ends, be sure to leave a tail at least ½" (1.3 cm) long hanging on the wrong side, especially if you're working with cotton or slippery yarns. Ends trimmed too close to the fabric will invariably work their way to the right side of the work. The wrong side will look a little chaotic, but that's a small price to pay for a right side that looks terrific!

WORKING WITH TEXTURED STITCHES

Many types of folk art and craft involve specific textures. From the sturdy and functional ash baskets of the Shakers to the simple and finer coiling of pine needles and raffia used by the Coushatta Indians of the southern United States, baskets offer wonderful and diverse textures. I also find texture ideas from vintage textiles—the lush softness of chenille bedspreads and the pronounced relief of trapunto quilting worked in a single color. These textures can be translated into knitting through ribs, cables, bobbles, lace, etc. As long as you remember that all textured stitches are simply manipulations of the knit stitch and the purl stitch, you can try new stitch patterns with confidence. You'll find hundreds of examples (and instructions for knitting them) of textured stitches in encyclopedias of stitch patterns. Check out the Bibliography (page159) for a few of my favorites.

However, don't feel you must be inspired by a texture to create a texture. Fiona Ellis deconstructed a color inspiration with the Bogolanfini Pullover (page 128) by re-creating the two-colored geometry of African mud cloth into a simple knit-and-purl pattern.

Keep in mind that textured stitch patterns usually work up at different gauges than stockinette stitch. The juxtaposition of knit and purl stitches in ribs causes the fabric to contract, the crossing of stitches in cables also causes the fabric to pull in and become narrower. Patterns such as lace that include yarnover increases have a tendency to stretch. Unfortunately, there's no way to predict exactly how these stitch patterns will affect your gauge—you'll have to knit a sample swatch of each one.

Véronik Avery used simple combinations of knit and purl stitches to create the embossed pattern in her classic Gansey Toque and Mitts (page 118). By using a plain, smooth yarn, she gave the texture sharp definition; by using a nontraditional color, she gave the design modern punch. In her Paisley Shawl (page 100), Kate Gilbert reinterpreted the rich, warm swirling colors of Indian paisley motifs into a bold graphic design by creating the motifs with lace stitches.

You can create even more depth and interest by combining color and texture. Di Gilpin successfully packs many design elements into a small space with her Grand Tour Waistcoat (page 38) by balancing intarsia patterning and subtle asymmetric texture. The broad striped and textured strap of Lisa B. Evan's Tribal Baby Carrier (page 80) not only mimics the African kente cloth that inspired it, but also adds necessary strength.

BOGOLANFINI PULLOVER
fiona ellis

EDGINGS

Edgings are a structural necessity to counteract knitted cloth's natural tendency to curl. But, you can turn these necessities into opportunities for adding a bit of folk style as well. Ribbed stitches are used worldwide to prevent curling and add a bit of snugness. Gayle Bunn turned the ribbing on her Algonquin Socks (page 96) into a continuation of the Fair Isle design by working a corrugated rib (the knit stitches are one color; the purl stitches are another).

Garter stitch is ideal for adding stability to an edge without changing the gauge or causing the stitches to draw in. By working garter stitch in multiple colors, you can add folkish appeal, as Leigh Radford did for her Urban Hand Warmers (page 110). Kristin Nicholas punctuated the stabilizing bands of garter stitch with narrow stripes of Fair Isle in her Sunny Flower Fez (page 68). Tara Jon Manning added a ribbon of multicolored intarsia squares between bands of garter stitch on the edges in her child's Tibetan Jacket (page 32).

Taking a cue from Dressmaking 101, Gayle Bunn used a hem to create the clean, flat finish on her Felt Appliquéd Skirt (page 90). Ann Budd added a playful picot edge to the hems of her Nordic Star pullover (page 86). Kate Gilbert used knit-cord to give a different kind of clean edge to her Paisley Shawl (page 100).

FELTING

Felting is a textile process that dates back centuries. From the Mongolian *ger* (tent) in the days of Genghis Khan to Tyrolean boiled wool jackets to Swedish slippers, felting is used in many folk traditions to create dense cloth that can be wind and water resistant. From a design perspective, it produces a sturdy fabric that doesn't ravel and that forms a good foundation for surface embellishment.

Gina Wilde knitted her Appalachian Gathering Basket (page 62) in Fair Isle color work, then sent it to the washing machine to felt it into a serviceable tote with an impressionistic design. Robin Melanson worked a felted version of traditional Norwegian footwear in her Bunad Mukluks (page 48) that are sturdy enough for outdoor wear. My Shibori-esque Neck Wrap (page 124) is simply a long rectangle embellished with crochet rings before hitting the hot water. Because felt won't ravel, the neck slit is simply cut into the fabric. All of the flowers and leaves on Gayle Bunn's Felt Appliquéd Skirt (page 90) are cut out of felted fabric and stitched in place—no need to worry about raveled edges.

URBAN HAND WARMERS
leigh radford

BUNAD MUKLUKS
robin melanson

EMBELLISHMENTS

Much of what we find appealing about folk textiles and arts are the details, many of which are added on after a piece is constructed. Whether it's a delicate bit of embroidery, a bold appliqué, or a whimsical tassel, a bit of added detail can add a lot of style.

Embroidery

Embroidery is a technique used by cultures worldwide. From humble, everyday pieces to those created for special ceremonies, colorful stitches are an important part of many textiles. Without the addition of colorful stitches and buttons, Pam Allen's All Buttoned Up cardigan (page 12) would be a plain red cardigan. Chain-stitched paisley motifs decorate the solid-color areas of Marilyn Webster's Indian Silk Pillow (page 114). Annie Modesitt added layers of color for a distinct three-dimensional look in her Shanghai Surplice (page 72). Instructions for all of these stitches and more are provided on pages 148–149.

Needle Felting

You can get a look that's similar to embroidery but with a more rustic appeal using needle felting, as Leigh Radford used to decorate her Urban Hand Warmers (page 110). Though not as common as embroidery, needle felting is gaining popularity as a way to add pictorial as well as geometric designs to wool and wool-blend knits. See the Bibliography on page 159 for more information.

Fringe, Tassels, and More

Ever notice how often folk crafts and textiles are topped off with tassels or fringe? Nomads commonly adorned their travel bags—smallish rugs folded in half and stitched into a pocket to hold belongings—with fantastically elaborate tassels, many of which incorporated beads and shells. Andean *chullo* caps (colorfully patterned with earflaps) are never without pom-poms, braids, or tassels (or all three!). In France, with the extravagances of Louis XIV, the most sumptuous tassels of tussah silk and wool appeared on virtually every piece of furniture in the Chateau de Versailles. For the most part, these whimsical additions are purely stylistic. Robin Melanson added tassels and just a bit of fringe to her Bunad Mukluks (page 48). Imagine tassels or fringe edging the Modern Quilt Wrap (page 24) or punctuating the top of the Sunny Flower Fez (page 64). Short or fat, long or lean, solid or multicolored—the possibilities are as varied as your imagination.

Buttons, Beads, and More

When you're looking for closures, consider ones that have a folk feel. To discretely emphasize the African theme of the Bogolanfini Pullover (page 128), Fiona Ellis picked buttons with zebra markings. Tara Jon Manning chose wooden toggle buttons that mimic traditional Tibetan brass beads to fasten her child's Tibetan Jacket (page 32). Keep in mind that as useful as they are as closures, a few carefully placed nonfunctioning buttons, beads, shells, or other findings can invoke the look of various cultures. The Haida and Tlingit peoples practiced their own folk style by adorning and personalizing wool blankets from the "white man" with mother-of-pearl buttons. In the highlands of Bolivia, knitters attached coins to their *monederos* (money pouches)—the reason, it is said, was to reflect both the maker's stitching talents and wealth. Pam Allen added buttons to punctuate the embroidery on her All Buttoned Up cardigan (page 12).

ALL BUTTONED UP
pam allen

TOP 10 TIPS FOR DESIGNING IN FOLK STYLE

1. Impart a spirit of fun and adventure in your designs.

2. Use color and texture freely.

3. Add a bit of your own personality.

4. Take time to measure your gauge in every stitch pattern you plan to use. If necessary, change the number of stitches or the needle size to prevent puckers when changing from one pattern to the next.

5. Experiment with new techniques by knitting a sampler of individual squares that you can later sew together into a patchwork pillow, afghan, or bedspread.

6. Learn from your mistakes—understanding what doesn't work in a design is as important as knowing what does.

7. Stir things up—many successful folk designs rely on contrast and tension.

8. If you love it, it's fabulous!

9. Develop a repertoire of knitting and embellishing techniques, then mix them up to create new combinations based on "old" favorites

10. "If you obey all the rules you miss all the fun."—Katharine Hepburn

Be adventurous when adding embroidery and embellishments—it's easy to remove anything you decide you don't like.

EMBROIDERY TECHNIQUES
BACKSTITCH

*Insert threaded needle at the right side of a stitch, then back out at the left side of a stitch two stitches away. Insert needle again between the first two stitches and bring it out two stitches away. Repeat from * as desired.

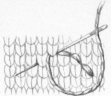

BLANKET STITCH

Working from left to right, bring threaded needle in and out of the knitted background, always keeping the needle on top of the working yarn.

BUTTONHOLE STITCH

Working into the edge half-stitch of the knitted piece, *bring tip of threaded needle in and out of a knitted stitch, place working yarn under needle tip, then bring threaded needle through the stitch and tighten. Repeat from *, always keeping the needle on top of working yarn.

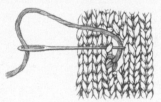

CHAIN STITCH

Bring threaded needle out from back to front at center of a knitted stitch. Form a short loop and insert needle back where it came out. Keeping the loop under the needle, bring needle back out in center of next stitch to the right.

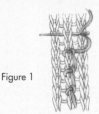

CROCHET CHAIN STITCH

Holding the yarn under the background, insert crochet hook through the center of a knitted stitch, pull up a loop, *insert hook into the center of the next stitch to the right, pull up a second loop through the first loop on the hook. Repeat from *.

CORAL KNOTS

Holding embroidery yarn to the right of and parallel to the desired line of stitching, *bring threaded needle into the knitted background at the right edge of one stitch and out again at the left edge of the same stitch (Figure 1). Pull the yarn through, insert the needle through the stitch just made from right to left, and pull the yarn snug (Figure 2). Repeat from * as desired.

Figure 1   Figure 2

CROSS-STITCH

Bring threaded needle out from back to front at lower left edge of the knitted stitch (or stitches) to be covered. Working from left to right, *insert needle at the upper right edge of the same stitch(es) and bring it back out at the lower left edge of the adjacent stitch, directly below and in line with the insertion point. Work from right to left to work the other half of the cross.

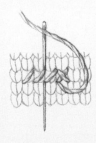

DAISY STITCH

Bring threaded needle out of knitted background from back to front, *form a short loop and insert needle into background where it came out. Keeping the loop under the needle, bring the needle back out of the background a short distance away (Figure 1). Beginning each stitch at the same point in the background, repeat from * for the desired number of petals (Figure 2; six petals shown).

Figure 1   Figure 2

DUPLICATE STITCH

Horizontal: Bring threaded needle out from back to front at the base of the V of the knitted stitch you want to cover. *Working right to left, pass needle in and out under the stitch in the row above it and back into the base of the same stitch. Bring needle back out at the base of the V of the next stitch to the left. Repeat from * for desired number of stitches.

Vertical: Beginning at lowest point, work as for horizontal duplicate stitch, ending by bringing the needle back out at the base of the stitch directly above the stitch just worked.

FRENCH KNOT

Bring threaded needle out of knitted background from back to front, wrap yarn around needle one to three times, and use your thumb to hold the wraps in place while you insert needle into background a short distance from where it came out. Pull the needle through the wraps into the background.

HERRINGBONE STITCH

Working on the right side of the desired line of stitching, *insert threaded needle into the knitted background, then out again one stitch below (Figure 1). Pull the yarn through, then bring the needle in and out of the knitted background in the same way two stitches up and one stitch to the left (Figure 2), pull the yarn through. Bring the needle two stitches up and one stitch to the right. Repeat from * as desired.

Figure 1   Figure 2

RUNNING STITCH

Bring threaded needle in and out of background to form a dashed line.

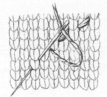

SATIN STITCH

Work straight stitches closely spaced and in graduated lengths as desired to completely cover the background.

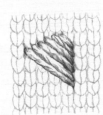

STEM STITCH

*Bring threaded needle out of knitted background from back to front at the center of a knitted stitch. Insert the needle into the upper right edge of the next stitch to the right, then out again at the center of the stitch below. Repeat from * as desired.

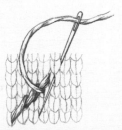

EMBELLISHMENTS

FRINGE

Cut several strands of yarn two times the desired fringe length, plus about 1" (2.5 cm) extra for the knot. Fold the yarn in half, insert a crochet hook from back to front into the knitted fabric, catch the fold of yarn and pull it through the knitting, pull the loose ends through the fold and tighten to secure.

POM-POM

Cut two circles of cardboard, each ½" (1.3 cm) larger than desired finished pom-pom width. Cut a small circle out of the center and a small wedge out of the side of each circle (Figure 1). Tie a strand of yarn between the circles, hold circles together and wrap with yarn—the more wraps, the thicker the pom-pom. Cut between the circles and knot the tie strand tightly (Figure 2). Place pom-pom between two smaller cardboard circles held together with a needle and trim the edges (Figure 3). This technique comes from *Nicky Epstein's Knitted Embellishments,* Interweave Press, 1999.

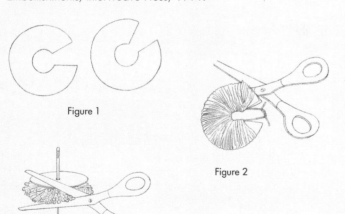

Figure 1

Figure 2

Figure 3

TASSEL

Cut a piece of cardboard 4" (10 cm) wide by the desired length of the tassel plus 1" (2.5 cm). Wrap yarn to desired thickness around cardboard. Cut a short length of yarn and tie tightly around one end of wrapped yarn (Figure 1). Cut yarn loops at other end. Cut another piece of yarn and wrap tightly around loops a short distance below top knot to form tassel neck. Knot securely, thread ends onto tapestry needle, and pull to center of tassel (Figure 2). Trim ends.

Figure 1

Figure 2

TWISTED CORD

Cut several lengths of yarn about five times the desired finished cord length. Fold the strands in half to form two equal groups. Anchor the strands at the fold by looping them over a doorknob. Holding one group in each hand, twist each group tightly in a clockwise direction until they begin to kink (Figure 1). Put both groups in one hand, then release them, allowing them to twist around each other counterclockwise. Smooth out the twists so that they are uniform along the length of the cord. Knot the ends (Figure 2).

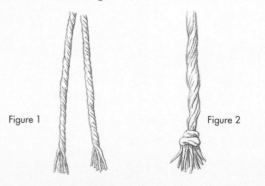

Figure 1

Figure 2

GLOSSARY OF TERMS AND TECHNIQUES

beg	begin(s); beginning		rep	repeat(s); repeating
BO	bind off		rev St st	reverse stockinette stitch
CC	contrast color		rnd(s)	round(s)
cm	centimeter(s)		RS	right side
cn	cable needle		sl	slip
CO	cast on		sl st	slip st (slip 1 st pwise unless otherwise indicated)
dec(s)	decrease(s); decreasing		ssk	slip 2 sts kwise, one at a time, from the left needle to
dpn	double-pointed needles			right needle, insert left needle tip through both front
foll	follow(s); following			loops and knit together from this position (1 st
g	gram(s)			decrease)
inc(s)	increase(s); increasing		St st	stockinette stitch
k	knit		tbl	through back loop
k1f&b	knit into the front and back of same st		tog	together
kwise	knitwise, as if to knit		WS	wrong side
m	marker(s)		wyb	with yarn in back
MC	main color		wyf	with yarn in front
mm	millimeter(s)		yd	yard(s)
M1	make one (increase)		yo	yarnover
p	purl		*	repeat starting point
p1f&b	purl into front and back of same st		* *	repeat all instructions between asterisks
patt(s)	pattern(s)		( )	alternate measurements and/or instructions
psso	pass slipped st over		[ ]	work instructions as a group a specified number
pwise	purlwise, as if to purl			of times
rem	remain(s); remaining			

BIND-OFFS

Standard Bind-Off

Knit the first stitch, *knit the next stitch (two stitches on right needle), insert left needle tip into first stitch on right needle (Figure 1) and lift this stitch up and over the second stitch (Figure 2) and off the needle (Figure 3). Repeat from * for the desired number of stitches.

Three-Needle Bind-Off

Place the stitches to be joined onto two separate needles and hold the needles parallel so that the right sides of knitting face together.

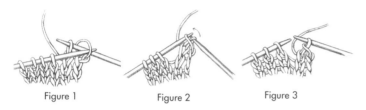

Figure 1   Figure 2   Figure 3

*Insert a third needle into the first stitch on each of two needles (Figure 1) and knit them together as one stitch (Figure 2), knit the next stitch on each needle the same way, then use the left needle tip to lift the first stitch over the second and off the needle (Figure 3). Repeat from * until one stitch remains on third needle. Cut yarn and pull tail through last stitch to secure.

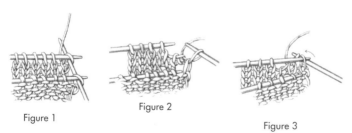

Figure 1

Figure 2

Figure 3

CAST-ONS

Backward-Loop Cast-on

*Loop working yarn and place it on needle backward so that it doesn't unwind. Repeat from *.

Cable Cast-On

Hold needle with working yarn in your left hand with the wrong side of the work facing you. *Insert right needle between the first two stitches on left needle (Figure 1), wrap yarn around needle as if to knit, draw yarn through (Figure 2), and place new loop on left needle (Figure 3) to form a new stitch. Repeat from * for the desired number of stitches, always working between the first two stitches on the left needle.

Figure 1   Figure 2   Figure 3

Long-Tail (Continental) Cast-On

Leaving a long tail (about ½" [1.3 cm] for each stitch to be cast on), make a slipknot and place on right needle. Place thumb and index finger of your left hand between the yarn ends so that working yarn is around your index finger and tail end is around your thumb and secure the yarn ends with your other fingers. Hold your palm upwards, making a V of yarn (Figure 1). *Bring needle up through loop on thumb (Figure 2), catch first strand around index finger, and go back down through loop on thumb (Figure 3). Drop loop off thumb and, placing thumb back in V configuration, tighten resulting stitch on needle (Figure 4). Repeat from * for the desired number of stitches.

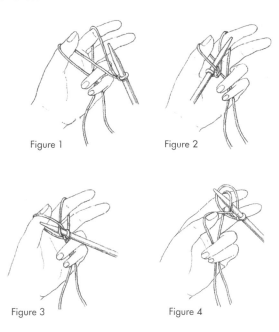

Figure 1   Figure 2

Figure 3   Figure 4

Provisional Cast-On

Make a loose slipknot of working yarn and place it on the right needle. Hold a length of waste yarn next to the slipknot and around your left thumb; hold working yarn over your left index finger. *Bring right needle forward under waste yarn, over working yarn, grab a loop of working yarn (Figure 1), then bring needle back behind the working yarn and grab a second loop (Figure 2). Repeat from * for the desired number of stitches. When you're ready to work in the opposite direction, place the exposed loops on a knitting needle as you pull out the waste yarn.

Figure 1   Figure 2

Crochet Chain Provisional Cast-On

With waste yarn and crochet hook, make a loose crochet chain (see page 159) about four stitches more than you need to cast on. With knitting needle, working yarn, and beginning two stitches from end of chain, pick up and knit one stitch through the back loop of each crochet chain (Figure 1) for desired number of stitches. When you're ready to work in the opposite direction, pull out the crochet chain to expose live stitches (Figure 2).

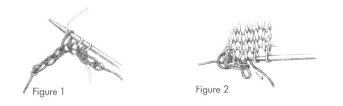

Figure 1   Figure 2

CROCHET

Crochet Chain (ch)

Make a slipknot and place it on crochet hook if there isn't a loop already on the hook. *Yarn over hook and draw through loop on hook. Repeat from * for the desired number of stitches. To fasten off, cut yarn and draw end through last loop formed.

Single Crochet (sc)

*Insert hook into the second chain from the hook, yarn over hook and draw through a loop, yarn over hook (Figure 1), and draw it through both loops on hook (Figure 2). Repeat from * for the desired number of stitches.

Figure 1

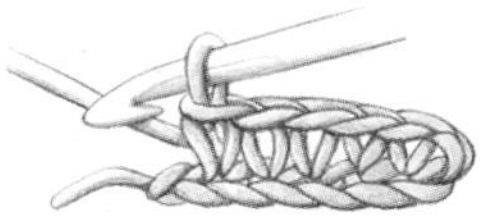

Figure 2

Slip-Stitch Crochet (sl st)

*Insert hook into stitch, yarn over hook and draw a loop through both the stitch and loop already on hook. Repeat from * for the desired number of sts.

DECREASES

Ssk

Slip two stitches individually knitwise (Figure 1), insert left needle tip into the front of these two slipped stitches, and use the right needle to knit them together through their back loops (Figure 2).

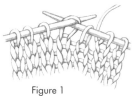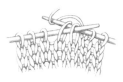

Figure 1

Figure 2

Sssk

Slip three stitches individually knitwise (Figure 1), insert left needle tip into the front of these three slipped stitches, and use the right needle to knit them together through their back loops (Figure 2).

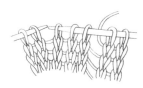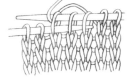

Figure 1

Figure 2

Ssp

Holding yarn in front, slip two stitches individually knitwise (Figure 1), then slip these two stitches back onto left needle (they will appear twisted) and purl them together through their back loops (Figure 2).

Figure 1

Figure 2

INCREASES

Make-One (M1)

Note: Use the left slant if no direction of slant is specified.

Left Slant (M1L): With left needle tip, lift the strand between the last knitted stitch and the first stitch on the left needle from front to back (Figure 1), then knit the lifted loop through the back (Figure 2).

Figure 1

Figure 2

Right Slant (M1R): With left needle tip, lift the strand between the needles from back to front (Figure 1). Knit the lifted loop through the front (Figure 2).

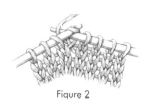

Figure 1

Figure 2

I-CORD

Using two double-pointed needles, cast on the desired number of stitches (usually three to four). *Without turning the needle, slide stitches to other end of needle, pull the yarn around the back, and knit the stitches as usual. Repeat from * for desired length

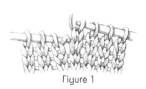

GRAFTING

Kitchener Stitch

Arrange stitches on two needles so that there is the same number of stitches on each needle. Hold the needles parallel to each other with right sides of the knitting facing up. Allowing about ½" (1.3 cm) per stitch to be grafted, thread matching yarn on a tapestry needle. Work from right to left as follows:

Step 1. Bring tapestry needle through the first stitch on the front needle as if to purl and leave the stitch on the needle (Figure 1).

Step 2. Bring tapestry needle through the first stitch on the back needle as if to knit and leave that stitch on the needle (Figure 2).

Step 3. Bring tapestry needle through the first front stitch as if to knit and slip this stitch off the needle, then bring tapestry needle through the next front stitch as if to purl and leave this stitch on the needle (Figure 3).

Step 4. Bring tapestry needle through the first back stitch as if to purl and slip this stitch off the needle, then bring tapestry needle through the next back stitch as if to knit and leave this stitch on the needle (Figure 4).

Repeat Steps 3 and 4 until no stitches remain on the needles, adjusting the tension to match the rest of the knitting as you go.

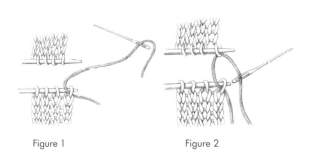

Figure 1

Figure 2

Figure 3

Figure 4

SEAMS

Mattress Stitch

Place the pieces to be seamed on a table, right sides facing up. Beginning at the lower edge and working upward as foll: *Insert threaded needle under one bar between the two edge stitches on one piece (Figure 1), then under the corresponding bar plus the bar above it on the other piece (Figure 2). *Pick up the next two bars on the first piece, then the next two bars on the other (Figure 3). Repeat from *, ending by picking up the last bar or pair of bars on the first piece.

To reduce bulk in the mattress-stitch seam, pick up the bars in the center of the edge stitches instead of between the last two stitches.

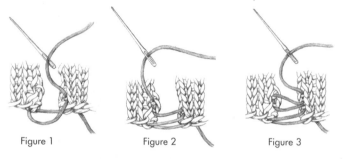

Figure 1   Figure 2   Figure 3

Whipstitch

Hold pieces to be sewn together so that the edges to be seamed are even with each other. With yarn threaded on a tapestry needle, *insert needle through both layers from back to front, then bring needle to back. Repeat from *, keeping even tension on the seaming yarn.

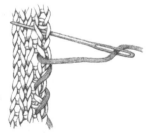

SHORT-ROWS

Short-Rows Knit Side

Work to turning point, slip next stitch purlwise (Figure 1), bring the yarn to the front, then slip the same stitch back to the left needle (Figure 2), turn the work around and bring the yarn in position for the next stitch, wrapping the slipped stitch with working yarn as you do so.

To hide the wrap on a subsequent knit row, work to the wrapped stitch, insert right needle tip under the wrap (from the front if wrapped stitch is a knit stitch; from the back if wrapped stitch is a purl stitch; Figure 3), then into the stitch on the needle, and knit the stitch and its wrap together as a single stitch.

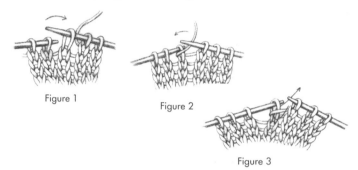

Figure 1   Figure 2   Figure 3

Short-Rows Purl Side

Work to the turning point, slip the next stitch purlwise to the right needle, bring the yarn to the back of the work (Figure 1), return the slipped stitch to the left needle, bring the yarn to the front between the needles (Figure 2), and turn the work so that the knit side is facing—one stitch has been wrapped and the yarn is correctly positioned to knit the next stitch.

To hide the wrap on a subsequent purl row, work to the wrapped stitch, use the tip of the right needle to pick up the wrap from the back, place it on the left needle (Figure 3), then purl it together with the wrapped stitch.

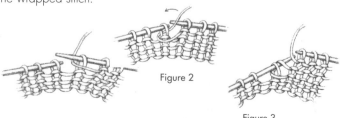

Figure 1   Figure 2   Figure 3

CONTRIBUTING DESIGNERS

Pam Allen is the creative director of Classic Elite Yarns. She is the former editor in chief of *Interweave Knits*, author of *Knitting for Dummies* and *Scarf Style*, and co-author of *Wrap Style* and *Lace Style*. After twenty-five years designing handknits, she's still learning something new about her craft on a regular basis.

Véronik Avery is the creative director for JCA Yarns. She has been designing for just four years and is currently working on her first book *Knitting Classic Styles*, due out in 2007. Véronik lives in Montréal, Quebec, with her husband and daughter.

Ann Budd is the former senior editor of *Interweave Knits* and is currently a book editor. She is author of *The Knitter's Handy Book* series and *Getting Started Knitting Socks*, and co-author of *Wrap Style* and *Lace Style*.

Gayle Bunn has been a knitter since learning from her grandmother at age six. She studied fashion design in Toronto with a focus on knitwear design in 1985. Since then, she has worked for numerous North American yarn companies and magazines.

Fiona Ellis is a British-trained knitwear designer who has been designing professionally for more than fourteen years. She enjoys marrying seemingly unrelated sources together in her designs. She is the author of *Inspired Cable Knits*, *Knitspiration Journal*, and *Inspired Fair Isle Knits*.

Lisa B. Evans is a landscape architect, devoted knitter, and mother of three. She founded *LB Evans Handknits* in 2001 with an innovative line of knitted handbags, backpacks, and totes, which is now represented by Westminster Fibers Inc. She is author of *Hip Graphic Knits*.

Kate Gilbert tried dozens of different arts and crafts before falling in love with knitting at the age of sixteen, and she hasn't put her needles down since. After living in New York and Paris, she has settled in Montreal where she spends her time knitting, teaching, spinning, and chasing her toddler.

Di Gilpin's inspiration has largely come from her response to the landscape of her Scottish homeland and her travels in the Himalayas. She balances her creative life between designing her distinctive knitwear and operating two inspiring knitting shops. Learn more about her workshops or join her Knitclub at digilpin.com.

Mags Kandis's love of travel (often only "armchair"), color, culture, texture, and discovery fuels her unique and identifiable knit designs. Mags is the head designer and consultant for Mission Falls Yarns.

Tara Jon Manning explores the use of knitting as a form of contemplative practice and the role of spirituality in art and craft. She contributes designs and writings to knitting magazines, books, and yarn companies. Tara has five books published on the subjects of knitting, knitting and meditation, and knitting and natural/organic fibers.

Robin Melanson is a freelance knitwear designer living in Toronto, Ontario. She finds inspiration in medieval literature and in the oral traditions of Early Irish heroic cycles, Icelandic saga, and Norse mythology. Robin is currently working on a book of innovative mitten and glove designs, to be published in 2008.

Annie Modesitt has a background in costume design that radiates throughout her knitting designs. She is the author of *Confessions of a Knitting Heretic*, *Knitted Millinery*, *Men Who Knit and the Dogs Who Love Them*, and *Twist & Loop: Dozens of Jewelry Designs to Knit and Crochet with Wire*. Visit her website at anniemodesitt.com.

Kristin Nicholas is a knitwear and stitchery author and designer who lives in the wilds of western Massachusetts. She and her husband and daughter raise a large flock of sheep, pigs, exotic chickens, border collies, and farm cats. Visit her website at kristinnicholas.com.

Leigh Radford is always looking for ways to stretch her knitting boundaries. Author of *AlterKnits: Imaginative Projects and Creativity Exercises*, and *One Skein: 30 Quick Projects to Knit and Crochet*, Leigh makes her home in the Pacific Northwest. To see more of Leigh's work, visit her website at leighradford.com.

Marilyn Webster's love for fiber arts began at age six when her mother taught her to knit while standing in line at Madame Tussaud's Wax Museum in London. A childhood spent in northern India fostered her passion for lush textiles and colors.

Gina Wilde is acclaimed for creating spectacular colors and blends of fiber in her line of handpainted natural yarns, Alchemy Yarns of Transformation (alchemyyarns.com). Her designs have appeared in *Hand Knit Holidays*, *The Knitter's Book of Yarn*, and *Interweave Knits*. She is currently working on a book about shibori knitting, due out in 2008.

SOURCES FOR YARNS

Alchemy Yarns of Transformation
PO Box 1080
Sebastopol, CA 95473
www.alchemyyarns.com
Sanctuary
Silk Purse

Aurora Yarns/Garnstudio
PO Box 3068
Moss Beach, CA 94038
www.garnstudio.com
In Canada:
Nordic Yarn Imports Ltd.
#301-5327-192nd Street
Surrey, BC V3S 8E5
Silke Tweed

Blue Sky Alpacas
PO Box 38
Cedar, MN 55011
www.blueskyalpacas.com
Alpaca-Silk

Brown Sheep Company
100662 County Rd. 16
Mitchell, NE 69357
www.brownsheep.com
NatureSpun Sport
Lamb's Pride Worsted
Cotton Fine

Classic Elite Yarns
122 Western Ave.
Lowell, MA 01851
www.classiceliteyarns.com
Miracle
Bazic

CNS Yarns/Mission Falls
100 Walnut, Door 4
Champlain, NY 12919
www.missionfalls.com
In Canada:
5333 Casgrain #1204
Montreal, QC H2T 1X3
1824 wool
1824 cotton

Crystal Palace Yarns
160 23rd St.
Richmond, CA 94804
www.straw.com/cpy
Cotton Chenille

Diamond Yarn
9697 St. Laurent, Ste. 101
Montreal, QC H3L 2N1
and
115 Martin Ross, Unit #3
Toronto, ON M3J 2L9
Canada
www.diamondyarn.com

Harrisville Designs
Center Village
PO Box 806
Harrisville, NH 03450
www.harrisville.com
New England Highland

JCA Inc./Reynolds
35 Scales Ln.
Townsend, MA 01469
www.jcacrafts.com
Reynolds Revue

Muench Yarns Inc./GGH
1323 Scott St.
Petaluma, CA 94954-1135
www.muenchyarns.com
In Canada: Oberlyn Yarns
GGH Scarlett

Oberlyn Yarns
5640 Rue Valcourt
Brossard, QC J4W 1C5
Canada
www.muenchyarns.com

The Fibre Company
North Dam Mill
Two Main St.
Biddeford, ME 04005
www.thefibreco.com
Terra

Westminster Fibers/Nashua/Rowan
165 Ledge St.
Nashua, NH 03060
www.westminsterfibers.com
In Canada: Diamond Yarn
Nashua Julia
Nashua Creative Focus Cotton
Nashua Creative Focus Worsted
Rowan Summer Tweed
Rowan Kidsilk Haze
Rowan Wool Cotton

Publications

Allen, Pam. *Scarf Style*. Loveland, Colorado: Interweave Press, 2004.

Allen, Pam, and Ann Budd. *Wrap Style*. Loveland, Colorado: Interweave Press, 2005.

Galeskas, Beverly. *Felted Knits*. Loveland, Colorado: Interweave Press, 2003.

Gibson-Roberts, Priscilla, and Deborah Robson. *Knitting in the Old Way: Designs and Techniques from Ethnic Sweaters*. Fort Collins, Colorado: Nomad Press, 2004.

Gillow, John, and Bryan Sentance. *World Textiles: A Visual Guide to Traditional Techniques*. London: Thames and Hudson, 2005.

Newton, Deborah. *Designing Knitwear*. Newtown, Connecticut: Taunton Press, New Ed., 1998.

Nicholas, Kristin. *Colorful Stitchery: 65 Hot Embroidery Projects to Personalize Your Home*. North Adams, Massachusetts: Storey Publishing LLC, 2005.

Walker, Barbara G. *A Treasury of Knitting Patterns*. Pittsville, Wisconsin: Schoolhouse Press, 1998.

Walker, Barbara G. *A Second Treasury of Knitting Patterns*. Pittsville, Wisconsin: Schoolhouse Press, 1998.

Internet Resources—Techniques and knitting information

Eunny Jang—detailed tutorials on traditional knitting techniques
www.eunnyjang.com/knit

Graph Paper Generator—enter your gauge and go
www.tata-tatao.to/knit/matrix/e-index.html

Knitty—patterns, techniques, articles, forums, and everything else knit
www.knitty.com

Knitter's Review—great source of all things new in knitting: yarns, tools, and gadgets. Weekly e-mail newsletter.
www.knittersreview.com

Internet Resources—Inspiration

Smithsonian Institute
www.si.edu

Textile Museum of Canada
www.textilemuseum.ca

Textile Museum (Washington, D.C.)
www.textilemuseum.org

Victoria and Albert Museum
www.vam.ac.uk

For more knitting patterns and techniques, join the community at knittingdaily.com—where life meets knitting—or subscribe to Interweave's magazines: *Interweave Knits* and *Interweave Crochet*.

knittingdaily

INDEX